HISTORY OF
CIVILIZATION
IN ENGLAND

MILESTONES OF THOUGHT

Henry Thomas Buckle

HISTORY OF CIVILIZATION IN ENGLAND

Summarized and abridged by
CLEMENT WOOD

Introduction by
HANS KOHN

FREDERICK UNGAR PUBLISHING CO.
NEW YORK

MILESTONES
OF THOUGHT
in the History of Ideas

General Editors

HANS KOHN
The City College of New York

SIDNEY HOOK
New York University

Copyright © 1964 by
Frederick Ungar Publishing Co., Inc.

Printed in the United States of America

Library of Congress Catalog Card No. 64-15688

INTRODUCTION

Henry Thomas Buckle is the author of one work only, and an unfinished work at that. Nevertheless, his place in the history of ideas, in the growth of the social sciences as sciences, is securely assured. He was one of those pioneers whose work is rarely read today but whose influence permeates all subsequent developments. His confidence in science and his methodical approach strike us today as mid-Victorian; for this reason alone the present re-edition, in view of the book's favorable reception in many countries, will be useful for any student of the thought and the public mind in the Western world during the mid-nineteenth century.

Yet the interest of this work goes much farther; in the twentieth century we have come to recognize the lasting contribution which Buckle made. Despite its time-conditioned inadequacies his book is, to quote Professor Crane Brinton in the *Encyclopaedia of the Social Sciences,* "one of the most important works in the history of the social sciences. Recent historiography is wholly in sympathy, if not with Buckle's methods, at least with his underlying assumptions as to the nature of history. In particular, his emphatic insistence on the study of the masses of men rather than of the exceptional individual has helped to create modern social history." Professor Brinton wrote these lines in 1930. Since then, history as a social science with the application of statistical and quantitative methods foreseen by Buckle has moved further in the direction he envisaged.

I

Henry Thomas Buckle (1822-1863) grew up in London as the son of a well-to-do merchant who was a staunch Tory and a devout member of the Church of England. Buckle's mother, whom he adored and whose death early in 1859 was the severest emotional blow of his life, came from a Calvinist Yorkshire family. The boy was of delicate health and thus received no regular schooling. But his unusual intelligence, his dedication to learning, his voracious reading and his facility in the acquisition of foreign languages, more than made up for his lack of formal scholastic training. His opinions of the educational institutions for the English elite was rather low, and for that time not without good reason: "What a war," he wrote, "Locke would wage against our great universities and public schools, where innumerable things are still taught which no one is concerned to understand, and which few will take the trouble to remember! . . . We often find what are called highly educated men, the progress of whose knowledge has been actually retarded by an education by which their reading has deepened their prejudices instead of dissipating them."[1]

When Buckle was eighteen years old, his father died and left him in very comfortable circumstances. He traveled for one year on the Continent, and it was then, though yet dimly, that he conceived the plan to "construct the science of history," to bridge the gulf separating the exact and the speculative sciences. At the same time he abandoned the religious and political traditionalism of his father and became a rationalist and a secular humanist.

As so many of his generation, he was influenced by the posi-

---

[1] *The History of Civilization in England,* vol. I., 2nd ed. (1858), p. 246. "Public schools" in England are, of course, the leading privately endowed preparatory schools which are not run for profit but as public trusts.

tivism of the French thinker August Comte (1798-1857). Comte tried to harmonize the contradictory trends that had shaken France from 1780 to 1830. He accepted the concept of history as the inevitable march of progress, a concept developed by the Marquis de Condorcet (1743-1794), who claimed to discover the laws of historical and social progress, laws as "necessary and constant" as those of the natural sciences. Even more did Comte, whose parents had been Catholic royalists, share the veneration of Count Joseph de Maistre (1753-1821) for time-honored order, for the precedence of society over the individual, of authority over rational criticism. Yet Comte was also influenced by Claude-Henri Count de Saint-Simon (1760-1825), who wished to replace the "discredited theology of feudalism" by scientific dogmas suitable for the new industrial age and a life of "positive utility." In 1830 Comte began the publication of his *Cours de philosophie positive,* in which he wished to discover, by scientific processes and historical verification, the laws governing the evolution of the human mind and of society, and to treat social facts like physical phenomena. Buckle called Comte "a living writer who has done more than any other to raise the standard of history."[2]

---

[2] *The History of Civilization in England,* vol. I, p. 5, note 1. But Buckle, with all his reverence for positivist science, was not blind to poetry and unique genius. He reserved his highest praise for Shakespeare, "the greatest of the sons of men," *ibid,* vol. II (1861), p. 42. "That [one] instance [of complete mastery], I need hardly say, is Shakespeare. No other mind has thoroughly interwoven the remote with the proximate, the general with the special, the abstract with the concrete. No other mind has so completely incorporated the speculations of the highest philosophy with the meanest details of the lowest life. Shakespeare mastered both extremes, and covered all the intermediate field. He knew both man and men. He thought as deeply as Plato and Kant. He observed as closely as Dickens and Thackeray. Of whom else can this be said?" *Essays* (New York: Appleton, 1863) p. 46f.

Much greater than Comte's influence on Buckle was that of John Stuart Mill (1806-1873). Buckle rejected Comte's reactionary views. He opposed his defense of Napoleon III's seizure of power in 1851 and his belief that the Czar "was the only statesman of Christianity." He fully shared Mill's radical Liberalism. He expressed his admiration of Mill in a lengthy essay ("Mill on Liberty"). He saw in him the only living Englishman who could scale the most exalted regions of thought and at the same time serve as a guide to the common transactions of daily life. Toward the end of his life Buckle remarked :"If Mill and I differ in opinion on any subject, I always have a latent belief that he is right and that I am wrong." Reading the first chapter of Mill's essay on "Utilitarianism," which appeared in 1861 in *Fraser's Magazine,* Buckle pointed to a passage and said, "No, if I had seen this, no matter where, I should have recognized the pen of Mill. He is the only man I have a very strong desire to know, and him I have never seen."[3]

He did not meet him, because after his return to England from the Continent, young Buckle devoted all his time and strength to his history of progress of the human mind, of civilization and society. He started on this work as a youth of twenty. The two introductory volumes which were to define and exemplify his method under the title *The History of Civilization in England* appeared in 1857 and 1861, when he turned forty. He published nothing before 1857, so as not to be distracted. His only "sport" was chess, wherein he achieved great distinction; he never married or established any ties with women. His veneration for his mother, however, and perhaps the example of J. S. Mill and Comte led him to select "The Influence of Women on the Progress of Knowledge" as the subject for his first lecture, which was delivered at the Royal Institution in March 1858. It

---

[3] Alfred Henry Huth, *The Life and Writings of Henry Thomas Buckle* (New York, Appleton, 1880) p. 345f.

was followed in the following year by a long essay, already mentioned, "Mill on Liberty," in which Buckle declared that if a jury of the greatest European thinkers were to declare who, among living writers, had done most for the advance of knowledge, they could hardly hesitate in naming Mill. "Nor can we doubt that posterity would ratify their decision."[4]

Buckle's long years of absorption in his book had exhausted his strength to such a degree that he fell ill in 1861. To regain his health, he started, in October of that year, on a voyage to Egypt and the Middle East. He died of typhoid fever in Damascus in May, 1862. His work remained incomplete. Yet the *New York Times* reviewer of the two volumes Buckle had finished, was right when he wrote "we owe him a profound debt of gratitude. His influence on the thought of the present age can not but be enormous, and if he gives us no more than we already have in the two volumes, he will still be classed among the fathers and founders of the Science of History."

II

Buckle himself stated the essence of his views on many occasions. Surveying the historiography of the past and of his own time, he complained that the ever-growing "mass of facts" had never been properly utilized. "In all the other great departments of investigation," he wrote, "the necessity of generalization is admitted by everyone, and we meet with noble exertions, based on specific facts, to reveal the laws under whose rule the facts stand. Historians, on the contrary, are so far from making this procedure their own as to be dominated by the strange thought

---

[4]   The two essays were published in *Fraser's Magazine for Town and Country* in April 1858 and May 1859. After his death Helen Taylor, Mill's stepdaughter and companion, edited Buckle's *Miscellaneous and Posthumous Works* in 3 vols., London 1872.

that their business is solely to recount transactions, enlivening these at the utmost with appropriate moral and political remarks." Different from "all higher tendencies of human thinking, History still lies in deplorable incompleteness and presents so confused and anarchical an appearance as were to be expected only in case of a subject with unknown laws or destitute as yet even of a foundation."

Buckle denied that the acts of men, and hence also of society, are the result either of accident or of supernatural influence. He believed that historiography, and thereby our understanding of social facts, had to come of age, had to be subject to definite laws and open to scientific investigation. His endeavor, a late fruit of the Enlightenment, was to place the progress of the human race upon secure foundations—the investigation of the laws of phenomena and the dissemination of the results of these investigations. "Before such an investigation can begin, a spirit of scepticism must be awakened, which then in turn furthers investigation and is furthered by it. The chief enemy of this movement, and hence the chief enemy of civilization is the paternal or guardianship spirit, the idea, namely, that human society can not prosper unless its affairs are watched over and protected at every step by State and Church, the State teaching men what to do, the Church what to believe."

The main lines of Buckle's approach were laid down in a letter to Lord Kintore of February, 1853. "You wish me to write a few words upon the object and tendency of that 'History of English Civilization' on which I have been now for some years engaged. It is very difficult to give in two or three lines a clear idea of so extensive a subject. But I may say generally that I have been long convinced that the progress of every people is regulated by principles—or, as they are called, laws—as regular and as certain as those which govern the physical world. To discover those laws is the object of my work. With a view to this, I propose to take a general survey of the moral, intellectual, and legislative peculiarities of the great countries of Europe; and I hope to point out the circumstances under which those peculiarities have arisen. This will lead to a perception of certain relations between the various stages through which each people have progressively passed. Of these general relations, I intend to make a particular application; and, by a careful analysis of the history of England, show how they have regulated our civilization, and how the successive and apparently the arbitrary forms of our opinions, our literature, our laws, and our manners, have naturally grown out of their antecedents. This is the general scheme of my work; and its merits, if it has any, will depend on the fidelity with which I carry that scheme into execution, and on the success of my attempt to rescue history from the hands of annalists, chroniclers, and antiquaries."

Buckle dedicated himself to his task with utmost scholarly scrupulousness. His methods and principles of work reveal the deep seriousness of his approach. When Alfred Huth, a young disciple of his, asked his advice about historical reading, Buckle remarked that "most people read too much and think too little"; and said that it was necessary to take copious notes while reading, and look them through very often. Of Prescott he observed that that part of his works which treats of the Netherlands was inferior to the Spanish part, because he had never taken the trouble to learn Dutch, and, therefore, had been unable to study those documents and works which were as yet untranslated. He advised me to read Lingard, not only because he was a good writer, but also because I lived in an atmosphere of Protestant opinion, and, therefore, ought to be careful to get acquainted with the opposite views."[5]

Buckle was not only a social scientist, emphasizing the fundamental value of political economy and statistics for an under-

---

[5] Huth, *op. cit.,* p. 301. William H. Prescott (1796-1859) wrote not only his well-known *Conquest of Peru* and *Conquest of Mexico,* but

standing of history, but he was a thorough democrat, stressing the part of the people, the common man, in making laws and history. The function of government, according to Buckle, is to express as best as it may the will of the people. In 1861 Buckle, like Mill, supported the Union in the War between the States. For him the people, or as it was said later, the masses are the moving force in history, not the great personalities. He emphasized that the history of the peasantry of any country had not yet been ever written and that without it the record of the doings of kings and nobles is mere chaff.

Buckle opposed the authoritarianism of Napoleon III and his appeal to French nationalism and grandeur, which Comte hailed. In 1861 Buckle refused a voyage to France in order to regain his health. In a conversation with Mr. Huth, he said, "I can not bear to see, what makes me miserable even to think about, a noble people under the heel of that great brigand—a people with such a literature. No, my indignation increases year by year as this reign goes on." He considered France, after England, the most civilized of all countries. "But," Mr. Huth urged, "in Germany there is more knowledge. A greater proportion of the German population are able to read and write even than the English." "Reading and writing is not knowledge in itself," he replied; "it is only a means to knowledge." "But you say in your first volume that you consider the German philosophers the first in the civilized world, and that Germany has produced a greater number of thinkers than any other country." "Certainly," he answered, "but if you look at the context you will see that I point out that their literature is the growth of

---

also a *History of the Reign of Ferdinand and Isabella* and a *History of Philip II,* of which three volumes appeared. John Lingard (1771-1851), an English Catholic historian and theologian, wrote *A History of England, from the First Invasion of the Romans to the Commencement of the Reign of William III* in 8 vols., 1819-1839.

but a century, has had hardly any influence on the people."[6]

Though Buckle was a rationalist humanist, he did not under-estimate the importance of emotions. "They are as much part of us as the understanding; they are as truthful; they are as likely to be right. Though their view is different [from that of the understanding], it is not capricious." And of the institution of priesthood, he wrote: "We may, if need be, remove some of its parts; but we would not, we dare not, tamper with those great religious truths which are altogether independent of it, truths which comfort the mind of man, raise him above the instincts of the hour, and infuse into him those lofty aspirations which, revealing to him his own immortality, are the measure and the symptom of a future life."[7]

Buckle knew that his new scientific approach would meet with much opposition. A scholar breaking new ground, and combating traditional views and prejudices, will find his recompense only within himself. "He must learn," Buckle wrote, "to care little for the sympathy of his fellow creatures or for such honors as they are able to bestow. So far from looking for these things, he should rather be prepared for that obloquy which always awaits those, who, by opening up new veins of thought, disturb the prejudices of their contemporaries. While ignorance, and worse than ignorance, is imputed to him; while his motives are misrepresented and his integrity impeached; while he is accused of denying the value of moral principles, and of attacking the foundation of all religion, as if he were some public enemy who made it his business to corrupt society, and whose delight it was to see what evil he could do; while these charges are repeated from mouth to mouth, he must be capable of pursuing in silence the even tenor of his way, without swerving, without pausing, and without stepping from his path to notice

---

[6] Huth, *op. cit.,* p. 328.
[7] *History of Civilization,* vol. II, p. 502; vol. I, p. 695.

the angry outcries which he can not but hear, and which he is more than human if he does not long to rebuke. These are the qualities and these the high resolves indispensable to him, who, on the most important of all subjects, believing the old road is worn out and useless, seeks to strike out a new one for himself, and in the effort not only perhaps exhausts his strength, but is sure to incur the enmity of those who are bent on maintaining the ancient scheme unimpaired. To solve the great problem of affairs, to detect those hidden circumstances which determine the march and destiny of nations, and to find in the events of the past a key to the proceedings of the future, is nothing less than to unite into a single science all the laws of the moral and physical world. Whoever does this will build up afresh the fabric of our knowledge, rearrange its various parts, and harmonize its apparent discrepancies."[8]

III

In view of the vastness of his enterprise, Buckle confined himself to a study of England; there the laws governing the progress of mankind and of civilization might be best studied because it is the country which has developed with least interference from outside. There the government interfered least with civilization or mental life. There, Buckle wrote, by applying "those methods of investigation which have been found successful in other branches of knowledge, and by rejecting all preconceived notions which would not bear the test of those methods, we have arrived at certain results, the heads of which it may now be convenient to recapitulate. We have seen that our actions, being solely the result of internal and external agencies, must be explicable by the laws of those agencies; that is to say, by

---

[8] Huth, *op. cit.,* p. 183. See also pp. 184-186 for a moving confession of Buckle's knowledge that he can finish only a small fragment of his plan, perhaps something on which future generations may build.

mental laws and by physical laws. We have also seen that mental laws are, in Europe, more powerful than physical laws, and that, in the progress of civilization, their superiority is constantly increasing, because advancing knowledge multiplies the resources of the mind, but leaves the old resources of nature stationary. On this account we have treated the mental laws as being the great regulators of progress; and we have looked at the physical laws as occupying a subordinate place, and as merely displaying themselves in occasional disturbances, the force and frequency of which have been long declining, and are now, on a large average, almost inoperative."

But the way in which the laws of the growth of civilization work in England can only be understood when the development in England is compared with that in other countries where the "protective" spirit, the interference with individual freedom of thought, has existed to a greater degree. Such countries, according to Buckle, are France, Germany, Spain, Italy, and Russia. Scientific method demands choosing a country for comparison with England where the conditions are most similar to those in England, except for the spirit of "protection." This country, Buckle believed, was France. "The French, as a people," he wrote, "have, since the beginning or middle of the seventeenth century, been remarkably free from superstition; and, notwithstanding the efforts of their government, they are very adverse to ecclesiastical power; so that, although their history displays the protective principle in its political form, it supplies little evidence respecting its religious form; while, in our own country, the evidence is also scanty." Another circumstance which operates on the intellectual progress of a nation is the method of investigation which its ablest men habitually employ. This method is either inductive or deductive. In Buckle's view, the two extremes of difference were undoubtedly Germany and the United States, the Germans being preeminently deductive and the Americans inductive. But Germany and America, he believed, are in so many other respects diametrically opposed to each other, that "it is expedient to study the operations of the deductive and inductive spirit in countries between which a closer analogy exists. . . . Such an opportunity occurs in the history of Scotland, as compared with that of England."

Thus Buckle confined himself to *The History of Civilization in England* as the first step toward a general history of civilization written in a scientific spirit. To classify the English development, he contrasted it with the history of France and of Spain to show the influence of the "protective" spirit, the authoritarian attitude of a government in guiding the thought of a people, on a "non-superstitious" people (France) and on Spain where the protective spirit took on a religious form. Buckle also contrasted the inductive method underlying English reasoning with the deductive method underlying reasoning in neighboring Scotland. Finally, he wished to discuss in a final volume of his introductory work the accumulation of thought in depth in Germany and its diffusion in breadth in the United States. This last part of the "introduction" to his history of civilization he was unable to finish.

Even in its unfinished form Buckle's "introduction" is a monumental giant of almost 1,200 pages. Though it is written with great clarity, it is much too long to be read today. In 1926 Clement Wood edited a skillful condensation of Buckle's work, omitting nothing of importance. This edition, long out of print, is here submitted to today's student as a "milestone of thought" in the growth of the social sciences.

HANS KOHN

Center for Advanced Studies
Wesleyan University

HISTORY OF
CIVILIZATION
IN ENGLAND

CONTENTS

CONTENTS

CHAPTER I

HISTORY: THE PHYSICAL LAWS

Resources for Investigating History: Statistics; Mental Laws and the Natural Sciences.—History has always been the most popular of the great branches of human knowledge. More has been written upon it than upon any other theme, and the general opinion is that the success of historians has been equal to their industry. The aggregate of materials is imposing. Political and military annals are ample, and well sifted; the histories of legislation and religion have been traced, and, in lesser degree, the chronicles of the progress of science, literature, the fine arts, useful inventions, and even the manners and comforts of the people. Antiquities have been exhaustively examined; philology, the science of words, has made rich contributions; and political economy has been raised to a science, throwing light on "the causes of that unequal distribution of wealth which is the most fertile source of social disturbance." Statistics of man's material interests and his moral peculiarities have been extensively compiled, and physical geography has been intensively gone into. A prodigious number of different tribes in all parts of the world have been visited and described by travellers, throwing light on the conditions of mankind in every stage of civilization, and under every variety of circumstances. Interest in these themes is insatiable, and is constantly increasing.

The use to which this material has been put is more

depressing. While the separate parts of man's history have been ably examined, few have attempted to combine these into a whole, and to study their connection with each other. In all other fields of inquiry, the necessity for generalization is universally admitted, and earnest efforts are made to rise from particular facts to the laws by which these facts are governed. To the contrary, historians hold the strange idea that their business is merely to relate events, occasionally enlivened by moral and political reflections. Historians, as a body, have never seen the necessity for the wide preliminary study which would enable them to grasp their subject in all its natural relations. One historian knows nothing of political economy; another, nothing of law; a third, little of church affairs; others, nothing of statistics, or of physical science: although all of these are indispensable to the adequate historian. The last hundred years shows slight improvement; but as yet scarcely anything has been done toward discovering the principles which govern the character and destiny of nations.

In regard to nature, events apparently irregular and capricious have been explained, and brought within certain fixed and universal laws. If human events were similarly studied, we have every right to expect a similar result. The history of the last two centuries shows that every generation demonstrates some events to be regular and predictable, which the preceding generation had declared to be irregular and beyond forecast. The marked tendency of advancing civilization is to strengthen our belief in the universality of order, of method, and of law. From this we must adjudge that any facts hitherto unpredictable will at some future time be explained. Two facts explain the attitude of historians: their inferiority as a class, and the greater complexity of the social phenomena with which their studies are concerned.

In physics, the regularity of events is assumed; in history it is at times actually denied, the historian holding that in the affairs of men there is something mysterious and providential. Our root problem, then, is: Are the actions of men, and therefore of societies, governed by fixed laws, or are they the result either of chance or of supernatural interference? Wandering tribes, living by hunting and fishing alone, would hold that chance determined their lives; an agricultural society, reaping what they sowed, would replace the philosophy of chance by that of natural connection. From these "there have respectively arisen the subsequent dogmas of Free Will and Predestination." "In every country, as soon as the accumulation of wealth has reached a certain point, the produce of each man's labor becomes more than sufficient for his own support; it is therefore no longer necessary that all should work; and there is formed a separate class, the members of which pass their lives for the most part in the pursuit of pleasure; a very few, however, in the acquisition and diffusion of knowledge." Such of these as study their own minds are influenced by the ideas current about them; thus Free Will and Predestination arise from current ideas of chance and necessary connection.

These opposite doctrines are safe and simple, easily understood, and even today an immense majority of men are divided between them; but "they have not only corrupted the sources of our knowledge, (they) have given rise to religious sects, whose mutual animosities have disturbed society, and have too often embittered the relations of private life." Advanced European thinkers are inclined to hold that both doctrines are wrong, or, at least, unsupported by evidence. For Predestination, or the idea that God has "from all eternity doomed to perdition millions of creatures yet unborn, whom His act alone can call into existence," a doctrine found alike in Calvin and early Catholic fathers, there has been brought forward no good evidence; it must be regarded scientifically as a barren hypothesis. Free Will rests on the metaphysical dogma of the supremacy of human consciousness. Two assumptions are needed to support it: that there is an independent faculty, called consciousness—an assumption by no means certain; and that its dictates do not err, which is obviously false.

The student of the science of history is not limited to either of these doctrines. "I shall expect him to concede merely (1) that when we perform an action, we perform it in consequence of some motive or motives; (2) that those motives are the results of some antecedents; (3) and that, therefore, if we were acquainted with the whole of the antecedents, and with all the laws of their movements, we would with unerring certainty predict the whole of their immediate results." Rejecting, then, both free will and predestination, Buckle proceeds from the fact that men's actions are determined by their antecedents, to the necessity that these actions have a character of uniformity; that is, that, under the same circumstances, the same results must follow. All antecedents must be in the mind, or out of it: so all actions must be the fruit of a double action, that of external phenomena upon the mind, and that of the mind upon the phenomena. "Thus we have man modifying nature, and nature modifying man; while out of this reciprocal modification all events must necessarily spring."

Our problem then is, which modification is the more important; since the more important should be studied before the other. The investigation of this Buckle bases upon statistics, or arithmetical tables, concerning the two classes of man's actions, the virtuous and the vicious. "The main object of legislation being to protect the innocent against the guilty, governments (began) to collect evidence regarding the crimes they were expected to punish." Statistics show that such a crowning act of vice as murder is committed with as much regularity, and bears as uniform a relation to certain known circumstances, as the movements of the tides and the rotations of the seasons. Each year witnesses the same approximate number of murders, committed with instruments in the same annual proportion. To take an even more isolated crime, less dependent upon outside interference, suicide is as uniform as murder, and must be "merely the product of the general condition of society." In a given state of society, a certain number of people must put an end to their own life.

Who shall commit the crime depends upon special laws, subordinate to the large social law. In London 240 is the annual average, particular conditions causing this to vary from 213 to 266.

Not only crimes may be forecast by statistics; but the number of marriages is determined, not by individual preferences, but by large general facts. "It is now known that marriages bear a fixed and definite relation to the price of corn"; they are regulated by the average earnings of the mass of the people. Amnesia, or forgetfulness, is similarly uniform: the number of letters misdirected annually in London remains approximately uniform. Thus statistics "has already thrown more light on the study of human nature than all the sciences put together." The connection of human actions and physical laws is undoubted; yet moralists and theologians, regarding the work of scientists as inferior, do not utilize its results, and frequently attack scientific inquiries as dangerous to the interests of religion, and as exaggerating the resources of man's mind. On the other hand, scientists, recognizing their constant progress, look down upon the more stationary position of the moralists and theologians. It is the business of the historian to unite these two branches of human endeavor into a consistent whole.

Physical Laws and Society.—The physical agents which most powerfully influence the human race are four: Climate, Food, Soil, and the General Aspect of Nature. The last of these produces its chief results by exciting the imagination, and by exciting those countless superstitions which are the great obstacles to human knowledge; it has caused variations in national characters, and peculiarities in national religions impossible to remove. Climate, food, and soil mutually affect each other, and should be considered together. Their earliest and most important result is the accumulation of wealth. For without wealth, there can be no leisure; "and without leisure, there can be no knowledge." Among an ignorant people, the accumulation of wealth will be regulated solely by the physical peculiarities of the country. Until later causes come into play, only two circumstances control here: (1) the energy and regularity of labor, and (2) the returns made to that labor by the bounty of nature. These two causes are the results of physical antecedents. The returns to labor are governed by the fertility of the soil, which is dependent on its chemical components, its natural water supply, and the heat and moisture in the air. The energy and regularity of labor, in their turn, depend upon the climate. Intense heat prevents active industry; only a temperate climate begets regular industry.

We observe these principles at work from the beginning in Asia. Civilization has always been confined there to that vast tract where the soil is rich, extending from the east of Southern China to the western coasts of Asia Minor, Phoenicia and Palestine. On the barren lands north of this, the uncivilized Mongolian and Tartar hordes have always wandered; and only when they entered upon the fertile plains, did they found those great monarchies in China, India, and Persia which vied with the ancient kingdoms. In their own arid country, the Arabs remained rude and uncultivated; their conquests, after the seventh century, of Persia, Spain, the Punjab, and most of India, soon transformed them into wealthy and civilized peoples, founding mighty empires. To the west of Arabia stretches the arid African desert: its eastern end, richly watered by the Nile, and extraordinarily fertile, permitted wealth to accumulate rapidly, knowledge to be cultivated, and Egyptian civilization to arise.

In the ancient world, then, the fertility of the soil was the most influential factor. In Europe, the climate was most powerful; and this cause affects both the capacity of the laborer for work, and the regularity of his habits. The fertile soil of Asia and Africa caused an abundant return of wealth; the happier climate of Europe caused more successful labor. The former case exhibited the effect of soil upon its produce—one part of nature upon another; the latter, the effect of climate upon the laborer—nature upon man. The first cause is less complicated, and came sooner into play, causing Asia and Africa to cradle civilization first. But this was not the best nor the most permanent civilization; for the only progress which is really effective depends, not on the bounty of nature, but on the energy of man. The powers of nature are limited and stationary; the powers of man are unlimited. Thus climate is more favorable to ultimate progress than the soil; the first gives wealth by stimulating labor, the second merely gives wealth.

After wealth is created, the question arises as to how it is to be distributed. This too is entirely governed by physical laws, when civilization begins. These laws have invariably kept a vast majority of the inhabitants of the fairest portion of the globe in a condition of constant and hopeless poverty. The distribution of wealth takes place between two classes, those who labor, and those who do not: the former being more numerous, the latter more able. The fund is created solely by the lower class, whose energies are directed by the superior skill of the upper class. The workman's reward is wages; the reward of the contrivers is called profits. The addition of a saving and lending class creates a third share of the fund, interest: so that the threefold division is, wages, profits, and interest. Wages being the price paid for labor, the rate of wages varies, like all commodities, according to changes in the market. If the supply exceeds the demand, wages will fall; "every increase in the number of the workmen will tend to lessen the average reward each can receive." In the long run, the question of wages is the question of population. Food tends most to increase the laboring classes; the population of a country having a cheap national food increases more rapidly than that of a country with an expensive food. In the former case it follows that wages will be lower.

Man's food produces two necessary effects: supply of animal heat, and repair of waste in his tissues. Body heat is kept up by food lacking nitrogen, called non-azotized food; the organism's incessant decay is repaired by azotized substances, in which nitrogen is always found. Men living in a hot climate need less of each kind of food, since the climate aids in supporting the body temperature, and their lesser exertions require less bodily repair. Other things being equal, the growth of population is more rapid in a hot country than a cold one. Moreover, in cold countries food is dearer. Bodily heat is achieved by oxygen, taken in through breathing, being combined with carbon from food. This combination must be in a definite proportion; and men in a cold country breathe air containing more oxygen, and the cold makes them inhale more frequently. This greater consumption of oxygen requires a greater consumption of carbon, from food. In polar countries, the chief foods, such as whaleoil and blubber, have an excess of carbon; tropical foods, fruit, rice, and other vegetables, have an excess of oxygen. Oils contain six times as much carbon as the fruits, and have little oxygen; starch, the most universal and important constituent in the vegetable world, is nearly half oxygen. Moreover, carbonized food is more costly. The fruits of the earth are abundant, and may be obtained without danger, and with little trouble; the highly carbonized foods consist of the fat, the blubber, and the oil of powerful and ferocious animals. Great risk and great labor are needed to obtain these. This requires a bolder and more adventurous character among the inhabitants of a cold country.

In Asia, Africa, and America, the ancient cultures were situated in hot countries; the rate of wages was low, and therefore the laboring class was very depressed. Europe saw the first civilization in a cold climate; here the wage of labor was increased. Only one European country, Ireland, has a cheap national food, that being the potato. So greatly did this depress Irish labor, that in 1837 the average wage was fourpence a day. Low wages of course cause a low social and political position for labor: the relation between the upper and lower classes depends on these same physical causes that have been indicated. India, seat of Asia's oldest continuing civilization, has in rice a cheap starchy food yielding an average return of at least sixty-fold. This has produced an upper class enormously rich, and lower classes miserably poor; with corresponding inequalities of social and political power. It is hard to measure India's wages, but, since profits, interest, and wages come from the same fund, if profits and interest are high, wages must be low. Interest in India, by the Institutes of Menu, 900 B. C., ranged from fifteen to sixty per cent. In 1810 A. D., Indian interest veered from thirty-six to sixty per cent. Rent (another measure like interest) in England is about one-fourth of the gross produce; in France, one-third; in the United States, much less. In India, the lowest rate of rent is one-half of the produce; at times, it hardly leaves seed for the next harvest. From this it follows that wages have been very low. Here, as everywhere, poverty produced contempt, and wealth produced power. The great mass of the people are called Sudras; if a member of this despised class presumed to sit beside one of his superiors, he was exiled or gashed in the buttocks; if he spoke of them with contempt, his mouth was to be burned; if he insulted them, his tongue was to be slit; if he listened to the reading of the sacred books, burning oil was to be poured into his ears; if he memorized them, he was to be killed. If he were murdered, the penalty was the same as for killing a dog, a cat, or a crow. The mere name of a laborer was lawfully an expression of contempt. Laws forbade laborers to accumulate wealth, and forever prohibited emancipation. Slavery was the natural state of the great body of the people. In no tropical country where wealth has accumulated, have the people escaped this fate. No such country ever shows the people turning upon their rulers, or conducting a war of classes, popular insurrection, or popular conspiracy. The democratic element is altogether wanting. Europe alone shows some approach to equality.

What is true of India, is applicable to Egypt, to Mexico, to Peru. Egypt has for its cheap national food dates, eaten both by men and animals. A cheap food, no necessary expense for clothes, conspired to effect a rapid multiplication of the people. Herodotus and Diodorus Siculus, the two ancient historians who treated of the land, point out the tyranny of the rulers, the slavery of the people. Between these two was an immense and impassable gap. The people were little better than beasts of burden. Thus 2,000 men were occupied for three years in carrying a single stone from Elephantine to Sais; the Red Sea Canal cost the lives of 120,000 Egyptians; to build one pyramid required 360,000 men for twenty years. In the New World, we do not find heat and moisture combined until we reach Mexico. In South America, the trade wind, added to the natural advantages, made nature in Brazil too powerful and formidable to permit civilization. Peru, however, like Mexico, was fitted by nature for an early civilization. Both Mexico and Peru had a cheap national food in maize, or Indian corn: in Mexico, this grain yields from 400 fold to 800 fold. Both potato and banana were also cheap starchy foods. Here too we find despotic power on the part of the upper classes, and slavery common to the lower. The law prescribed, for the poor man, what trade he was to follow, what dress he was to wear, what wife he was to marry, what amusements he was to enjoy. Tyrants and slaves, and a caste system—found alike in Egypt, India, Peru, and, in substance, in Mexico. One royal residence in Peru required, for its construction, 20,000 men, for fifty years; one in Mexico cost the labor of 200,000 men. Such societies, being divided internally, could not withstand external pressure: internal decay and degeneracy prepared the way for foreign conquest of all of these ancient kingdoms.

Aspects of Nature and Man's Imagination.—In such ways were the great civilizations outside of Europe affected by food, soil, and climate. These were concerned chiefly with the accumulation of wealth; the aspects of nature generally, with the accumulation and distribution of thought. These aspects of nature may be divided into those which are most likely to excite the imagination; and those which address themselves to man's understanding, and the logical operations of his intellect. Usually the understanding is too weak to curb the imagination, and control its dangerous license. As civilization advances, the intellect gains more authority; yet even today the imagination has far too much power.

Whatever natural phenomena inspire terror, or great wonder, tend especially to inflame the imagination. Man, in such cases, contrasting himself with the majesty of nature, becomes painfully aware of his insignificance. A sense of inferiority steals over him. When, on the other hand, nature seems feeble, man regains confidence: he can experiment on such phenomena, observe them minutely, and ultimately reduce them to the laws by which they are governed. From this standpoint, it is remarkable that all the great early civilizations were situated near the tropics, where nature is most dangerous to man. In Asia, Africa, and America, the external world is more formidable than in Europe. Not only great mountains and oceans, deserts and rivers, but earthquakes, tempests, hurricanes, pestilences, are more prevalent. The very atmospheric change that precedes an earthquake has a direct physical tendency to impair the intellect, and, of course, by producing utter terror, turns men from understanding to superstitious fancies. What is stranger, repetition, instead of blunting the feeling, strengthens it. In Peru, where earthquakes are frequent, each succeeding visitation increases the general dismay; the mind is kept timid and anxious, the imagination aroused, and a belief in supernatural interference encouraged.

In Europe, earthquakes and volcanic disturbances are more frequent and destructive in Italy, Spain, and Portugal than elsewhere in Europe; and these are precisely the countries where superstition is most rife, and the superstitious classes most powerful. Here the clergy first established their authority, here the worst corruptions of Christianity took place. The fine arts are addressed most to the imagination, the sciences to the intellect: these countries lead the rest of Europe in painting, sculpture, and poetry, while they lag in the sciences. Among more backward people, not only is supernatural interference seen in such manifestations of nature as have been referred to, but the danger is at times actually worshipped. Thus some inhabitants, from superstitious feelings, refuse to destroy wild beasts and noxious reptiles, and instead worship them. In the older civilizations mentioned, subject to devastating animals, hurricanes, tempests, and earthquakes, the people were possessed with a spirit of reverence, instead of a spirit of inquiry: supernatural causes were believed in, instead of natural causes being investigated.

Here pestilences were thought to be manifestations of the divine anger. Moreover, these tropical regions were more unhealthy than temperate Europe. All these causes conspired to increase the authority of the imagination, and weaken the authority of reason. This in turn affected the literature, religion, and art of these countries. For instance, in India, scarcely any attention has been paid to prose composition; all the best writers devoted themselves to poetry. Grammar, law, history, medicine, mathematics, geography, are expressed in regularly versified poems. In spirit, everything is calculated to set the reason of man at open defiance. Imagination, luxuriant even to disease, runs riot on every occasion. Take that aspect of the undue respect for past ages evidenced in longevity tables. Christian and Hebrew sources have gone so far as to give early man a life of almost a thousand years; Indian records state that, in the early times, the duration of life of the common man was 80,000 years; several early poets lived to be 500,000 years old. One king and saint was 2,000,000 years old when elevated to the kingship; he reigned 6,300,000 years; resigned his empire, and lingered on for 100,000 years more. All chronologies are similar: the Institutes of Menu, certainly less than 3,000 years old, are said to have been revealed to man some 2,000,000,000 years before the present era.

Contrast this with Greece, where nature is feebler, smaller, and in every way less threatening than in India. The climate was healthy, earthquakes less frequent, hurricanes less disastrous, wild beasts less abundant. In India, nature intimidated man; in Greece, its impotence encouraged him. Here natural causes began to be studied, and physical science first

became possible. Accordingly, the religion differed from that of India. India's great god Siva was a hideous being, encircled by a girdle of snakes, with a human skull in his hand, and wearing a necklace of human bones. He had three eyes, wandered about like a madman, wore over his left shoulder the deadly cobra. His wife Doorga, or Kali, had a body of dark blue, with red hands, to show her appetite for blood. She had four arms, a protruding tongue, a belt of severed hands, and a necklace of ghastly human heads. All the gods were monstrous, as Vishnu with four hands, Brahma with five heads. The gods of Greece might be stronger or more beautiful than men, but they were still men. They had the traits, the trades even, of men. Greek religion elevated heroes to semi-divinity; in religions outside Europe, since man was so insignificant, this is never met with. The Greeks had more respect for human powers; the Indians, for superhuman. Religions in Mexico, Peru, Egypt, were similar to the Hindu religion of terrors. The dangers of the tropic civilizations emphasized the infinite, the safety of European civilizations suggested the finite.

CHAPTER II

HISTORY: THE MENTAL LAWS

Methods for Discovering Mental Laws.—In civilizations out of Europe, the powers of nature have been far greater than in those of Europe; and these powers have worked immense mischief. One division has caused a ruinous division of wealth, the other has caused a harmful division of thought, by unduly inflaming the imagination. Outside of Europe, the tendency has been to subordinate man to nature: in Europe, to subordinate nature to man. Thus in a European country like France or England, our principal study must be man; since the weakness of nature has meant that every step in man's progress has increased the dominion of the human mind over the agencies of nature. Even in our most developed countries, the pressure of nature is still immense; but this decreases with each succeeding generation. The duration of life is longer, the number of inevitable dangers fewer, in spite of the closer human contacts. Thus in the history of Europe, the primary cause of its superiority over the rest of the world lies in the encroachment of the mind of man upon the organic and inorganic forces of nature.

In Europe, it seems that there is nothing that man has feared to attempt. Invasions of the sea have been repelled, and whole provinces, as Holland, have been rescued from its grasp; mountains have been cut through, and levelled into roads; sterile soils have been made fertile by chemistry; and electricity has been harnessed to convey man's thoughts and to obey his mere whims. Cruel diseases, such as the plague and leprosy, have been rooted out; wild beasts and birds of prey have been banished; famines have ceased. In Asia and

14

elsewhere, trade and commerce were determined by the rivers and harbors; in Europe, where no rivers were, canals were made, and where no harbors existed, artificial ones were created. The richest countries are no longer those where nature is most bountiful, but those where man is most energetic. In Europe the population of the towns is everywhere outstripping that of the country. To summarize the whole process, the advance of European civilization is characterized by a diminishing influence of physical laws, and an increasing influence of mental laws.

We are in possession of no evidence that the powers of nature have ever permanently increased; we have abundant evidence that the resources of the human mind have become more powerful, more numerous, and more able to grapple with the difficulties of the world without. If the measure of civilization is the triumph of mind over external agents, it becomes clear, that of the two classes of laws which regulate the progress of mankind, the mental class is more important than the physical. Our problem now has become simplified: a discovery of the laws of European history is resolved, in the first instance, into a discovery of the laws of the human mind. These mental laws will be the ultimate basis of the history of Europe; the physical laws will be treated as of minor importance, whose disturbances have for several centuries been perceptibly diminishing.

The metaphysical method consists in each observer studying the operations of his own mind. This is the direct opposite of the historical method; the historian studies many minds, the metaphysician, one. By the metaphysical method no discovery has yet been made in any branch of knowledge. All we know has come from studying phenomena, from which casual disturbances have been removed, the laws remaining as an obvious residue. This can only be done by observations so numerous as to eliminate the disturbances; or by experiments so delicate as to isolate the phenomena. One of these alternative methods is essential to all inductive science, or science that reasons from facts to general principles; but neither of them does the metaphysician obey. He can not isolate the phenomenon, since his own mind continues subject to external events; he refuses to enlarge his survey, since his method consists in the study merely of his own mind.

The two metaphysical methods are studying the observer's sensations, and studying his ideas. These methods have always led to conclusions diametrically opposed to each other. Thus in studying the idea of space, the idealist, or student of ideas, says that this can not come from the senses, which supply only what is limited and contingent; whereas the idea of space is infinite and necessary. But the sensualist, or student of sensations, holds that the idea of space comes from the ideas of objects, obtained by the senses; we only hold it necessary by association with sensations of objects, and our notion of infinite comes from the idea of continual addition to lines, or surfaces, or bulks, the three modifications of extension. Metaphysical ideas of time, cause, personal identity, and substance, differ as sharply, from the two standpoints of students of ideas and sensations. Idealists say that men have essentially the same notion of the good, the true, the beautiful; sensationalists affirm that there is no such standard, since changes in men's bodies and external sensations determine these.

Yet with these two points of view, the resources of metaphysics have been exhausted. Both parties confine their study to the mind of the observer; each process is equally plausible, and viewed from the outside, barren of results. The confusion they have achieved is only equal to the confusion in the study of religion caused by theologians. There must be some fundamental error in the manner in which these inquiries have been prosecuted; mere observation of our own minds, and the rude experiments we may make upon them, can never raise psychology to a science. Only a comprehensive investigation of history can achieve this.

Moral and Intellectual Laws.—The only remaining method by which mental phenomena may be studied, is by studying the actions of mankind at large. Take such a problem as the proportion in the births of the sexes, for illustration. It has always been suspected that the male and female births are approximately equal. It was known further that this physical result of physical antecedents must have its antecedents located in the parents themselves. The physiologist sought the laws governing this proportion in individual bodies, and in the laws which regulate the unions of the parents. This method, in spite of the aid of anatomy, was utterly useless: but the method of statistics established that there are 21 boys for every 20 girls, over all the areas collectively studied. What concerns us is the method in which the discovery was made: not by individual experiments, but by a survey of society as a whole.

Mental progress is twofold: moral, and intellectual; the first relating to our duties, the second to our knowledge. It is clear that progress involves both; since a people are not really advancing, if their mentality is accompanied by increasing vice, or their virtue by increasing ignorance. Which of these elements of mental progress is the more important? This progress does not lie in the faculties themselves; we cannot safely assume that there has been any permanent improvement in the moral or intellectual faculties of man, nor have we decisive ground for saying that these faculties are likely to be greater in an infant born in the most civilized part of Europe, than in one born in the wildest region of a barbarous country. We mean, then, not a progress of capacity, but of opportunity; not of internal power, but of external advantage. Thus the entire mental atmosphere governs. It is hence clear that moral and intellectual conduct is regulated by the moral and intellectual notions prevalent in their own time and place. Some rise above these notions, some sink below them: an immense majority of men must always remain in a middle state, neither very foolish nor very able, neither very virtuous nor very vicious, slumbering on in a peaceful and decent mediocrity, adopting without inquiry the time's opinions, and noiselessly conforming to the standard of morals and knowledge common to the age and land in which they live.

This standard, however, is constantly changing. What in one period is attacked as a paradox or a heresy, in another period is welcomed as a sober truth; while a new novelty has come in for attack and later espousal. Applying this test to moral motives, we at once see how small is the influence these have exerted over the progress of civilization. Nothing in the world has undergone so little change as the great moral dogmas. "To do good to others; to sacrifice for their benefit your own wishes; to love your neighbor as yourself; to forgive your enemies; to restrain your passions; to honor your parents; to respect those who are set over you; these, and a few others, are the sole essentials of morals; but they have been known for thousands of years, and not one jot or tittle has been added to them." The system of morals in the New Testament was original in no one particular; which shows Christianity's consonance with the moral ideals of men in all ages.

Contrasted with this stationary aspect of moral truths, is the dynamic condition of intellectual truths. All great moral systems have been fundamentally the same; all great intellectual systems have been fundamentally different. Not only is the intellectual principle more progressive than the moral, it is also more permanent in its results. Intellectual acquisitions in every country are written down, treasured up, and used by distant posterity; good moral deeds, of private and retiring character, often perish with the doer. Moral excellence is more amiable; yet it is far less active, less permanent, and less productive of real good. The result of the most disinterested philanthropy is short-lived; and, when it takes the form of founding great public charities, such institutions invariably fall, first into abuse, then into decay, and in the end are either destroyed or perverted from their original intention.

These conclusions are unpalatable; worse than that, they cannot be refuted. The superiority of intellectual acquisitions over moral feelings is everywhere apparent. No ignorant man, with good intentions, ever failed to do far more evil than good. If you diminish his sincerity, you likewise diminish the evil he works. The history of religious persecutions proves this beyond doubt. "To punish even a single man for his religious tenets, is assuredly a crime of the deepest dye;" to punish a whole sect is "one of the most pernicious and foolish acts" possible. Yet religious persecutors have been men of pure intention and unsullied morals. Such men are not bad, but ignorant; ignorant of the nature of truth, ignorant of the consequences of their own acts. Morally, their motives were unimpeachable.

Among the Roman persecutors of the Christians, we find the names of the best men who sat on the throne, such as Marcus Aurelius; you do not find the two most depraved emperors, Commodus and Heliogabalus. Similarly, the religious sincerity of Spain, unparalleled in Europe, has been the means of encouraging religious persecutions. The supporters of the barbarous Inquisition were not hypocrites, but enthusiasts. Hypocrites are, for the most part, too supple to be cruel. In Spain, hatred of heresy became a habit, and persecution of it a duty. The bitterest enemies of the Inquisition never attacked the sincerity of the most barbarous Inquisitors. "It is to the diffusion of knowledge, and to that alone, that we owe the comparative cessation of what is unquestionably the greatest evil men have ever inflicted on their own species." Worse than the known victims were the unknown victims of the persecution—men driven to falsehood and hypocrisy to escape death, greatly increasing the gross amount of vice and error. Compared to this, all other crimes are of small account.

Next to this evil is the practice of war. "That this barbarous pursuit is, in the progress of society, steadily declining, must be evident, even to the most hasty reader of European history." Even the ancients knew all that we know of the moral evils of war. They knew that defensive wars are just, and that offensive wars are unjust. Every important addition made to knowledge increases the power of the intellectual classes; and their antagonism to the military classes is evident. Barbarous countries rank a man by the number of enemies he has killed: from this frightful debasement, the intellectual and pacific classes slowly arise; trade, commerce, manufactures, law, diplomacy, literature, science, philosophy, become organized, and oppose the warlike spirit. The present war (the Crimean war, 1855) arose, not between two civilized powers, but between Russia and Turkey; in this France and England drew the sword, not for selfish purposes, but to protect civilization against a barbarous foe. Yet Russia is warlike, not because its inhabitants are immoral, but because they are unintellectual; the intellectual classes lack influence, the military class is supreme. In England, on the other hand, a love of war is, as a national taste, utterly extinct. With the decline of the military classes in reputation, goes their decline in ability. In a backward society, the ablest intellects go into the military; today a backward boy is either made a soldier or a clergyman. As society advances, the ecclesiastical spirit and the military spirit never fail to decline.

In ancient Greece the most successful statesmen, and the ablest philosophers, orators, tragic dramatists, historians, and poets were warriors. In the modern world, all Europe has not produced ten soldiers who reached the first class as writers or thinkers. Cromwell, Washington, and Napoleon are the only modern warriors also fit to govern a country. England's Marlborough was a man of frivolous pursuits, and miserably ignorant, as well as doubly a traitor; Wellington, in politics, was an obstinate opponent of all reforms, even the most essential. The warlike spirit has been reduced by the invention of gunpowder, which made the footsoldier equal to the knight; and by the discoveries of political economy, which destroyed the iniquitous idea that a nation's wealth consisted of gold. Adam Smith's "Wealth of Nations" in 1776 ended this fallacy; and he, "by the publication of one single work, contributed more toward the happiness of man, than has been effected by the united abilities of the statesmen and legislators of whom history has preserved an authentic account." Before his book appeared, governments felt they could only prosper as they drained other countries of gold; today it is understood that prosperity arises from the ease with which a nation gets rid of those commodities which it can produce most cheaply, and receives in return those commodities which it can produce only at great cost, but which other nations can produce cheaply. "The result is, that the commercial spirit, which formerly was often warlike, is now invariably pacific."

The third cause of the decay of the warlike spirit is the application of steam to transportation. This, by bringing nations closer, has ended national misunderstandings, such as the English idea that all French women are unchaste, and all Frenchmen were cowards, infidels, and frog-eaters; and the French idea that all Englishmen were surly brutes living in eternal fog, constantly committing suicide, especially in November, when thousands annually shot and hung themselves. Virtues are more frequent than vices; otherwise, as we get to know our neighbors, we should hate them; since we may hug our own vices, but not our neighbors'. Only the intellectual process could thus have diminished religious persecution and war; the operation of moral feelings was impotent. The progress Europe has made from barbarism to civilization is entirely due to its intellectual activity. Virtues and vices counteract each other; the "gigantic crimes of Alexander or Napoleon become after a time void of effect, and the affairs of the world return to their former level." Above this ebb and flow of history is the far higher movement of intellectual progress.

Influence Exerted by Religion, Literature, and Government.
—In the amount and diffusion of intellectual knowledge, then, we must seek the conditions which regulate the progress of modern civilization; remembering that physical phenomena and moral principles cause great aberrations in short periods, but in long periods correct and balance themselves. Thus over a long stretch of time the intellectual laws act uncontrolled

by these inferior and subordinate agents. The writers of history have ignored these major matters, and have given us instead personal anecdotes of kings and courts, of what this minister did and that minister thought, and, worst of all, long accounts of campaigns, battles, and sieges, useless because they furnish no new truths, nor do they supply the means by which truth may be discovered. The historian today must collect the important facts, as well as generalize from them. He must be mason as well as architect; he must excavate the quarry, as well as scheme the edifice. This consideration has dictated that the original plan, of a history of general civilization, must be replaced by the history of the civilization of a single people.

By thus restricting the field covered, the attempt loses something of its original value. As the field is narrowed, the greater becomes the uncertainty of the average. Foreign interferences of every kind, which equalize each other in universal history, are apt to disturb the general march of one country, and thus render the movements of civilization more difficult to calculate. The country selected is England, for certain definite reasons. The history of any people becomes more valuable, in proportion as their movements have been least disturbed by outside agencies. To simplify complications is, in all branches of knowledge, the first essential of success. Thus the importance of the history of a country depends, "not upon the splendor of its exploits, but upon the degree to which its actions are due to causes springing out of itself." We therefore look for a people neither affected by foreign influence nor by the peculiarities of their rulers—a task obviously impossible. But this has been more true of England, during the last three centuries, than of any other country. Of all the European countries, England is the one where, during the longest period, the government has been most quiescent, and the people most active; where popular freedom has been settled on the widest basis; where religious persecution is least known, dissent most common, and the profession of heresy least dangerous. Owing to its island formation England was, until the middle of the last century, little visited by foreigners: thus we have been least of all the nations affected by the authority of government, and the influence of foreigners.

In the sixteenth century, our nobles began to travel abroad; but foreign nobles did not then visit us. In the next century, we had such visitors; yet there were many of our cities in which only Englishmen ever set their feet. The French influence after the restoration of Charles II affected only a small and insignificant part of society, the court circles; nor did it greatly affect the two most important classes, the intellectual class and the industrious class. From France we have borrowed nothing essential, nothing by which the destinies of nations are permanently altered. To the contrary, the French Revolution of 1789 was mainly instigated by eminent leaders who had learnt in England that philosophy which set the other land on fire.

When the claims of other nations to be studied instead of England are investigated, Germany at once comes to mind. Since the middle of the eighteenth century that land has produced more profound thinkers than the other countries put together. But the protective spirit is more rampant there than in France; the government is constantly interfering with the people. The German literature owes its origin to the scepticism that preceded, in France, the Revolution; and certain conditions have stimulated the growth of a literature produced more rapidly than the country needs. Thus in no nation in Europe do we find such an interval between the highest and the lowest minds. The German philosophers lead the civilized world; the German people are more superstitious, prejudiced, and ignorant than are the inhabitants of France or England. Thus there is no sympathy between the high intellects and the rest of the country. The literature is marked by great boldness of inquiry and disregard of traditions, but also by an absence of practical knowledge, and an indifference to earthly interests.

America has also been suggested. There we have "few

men of great learning, and few men of great ignorance";
contrary to the condition in Germany, the speculative and
the practical classes are there altogether fused. Thus there
are no new discoveries, new philosophies, new means by which
the boundaries of knowledge are to be enlarged. The stock of
American knowledge is small, but it is spread through all
classes; the stock of German knowledge is large, but it is
confined to one class. The latter country fails in diffusion of
knowledge; the former, in accumulation. From such motives,
and not at all from those motives dignified with the name
of patriotism, "I have determined to write the history of my
own country, in preference to that of any other." Yet since
no one nation can give the laws of society, this introduction
is furnished. This has led us to the conclusion that national
progress, in connection with popular liberty, could have
originated in no part of the world except Europe. Since in
Germany the accumulation of knowledge has proceeded more
rapidly than in England, we shall study that accumulation in
Germany; since Americans have diffused their knowledge
more amply than we, we shall study that diffusion in America.
Since France is the most civilized country in which the protective spirit is powerful, we will study that spirit there, by
showing the injury it has effected on an able and enlightened
people. It will be pointed out how the French Revolution
was a reaction against the protective spirit; and we will see
how the intellect of one country reacted upon another, in the
English influence upon the coming of the Revolution. To
show a country uniting the protective spirit with superstition,
we shall survey the history of Spain. Again, there are only
two methods of intellectual investigation, the deductive and
the inductive. Germany and America respectively illustrate
these two tendencies fully; but, since these countries are so
diametrically opposed in so many ways, it seems more advisa-
ble to study the closer analogy of Scotland and England, the
first preeminently deductive, the second inductive.

Deduction, or reasoning from principles down to facts,
which Scotch thinkers follow, neglects those lower generaliza-

tions which are the only ones that the lower classes can understand; hence the lower classes are separated from such an intellectual class by a wide chasm. The contrary is true of a country, like England, using the inductive method, which reasons up from facts to general principles. Before entering upon the introduction proper, it is necessary to notice three forces, religion, literature, and government, which many hold are the prime movers in human affairs. It is clear that, if a people is left to itself, their religion, their literature, and their government would be, not the cause of their civilization, but the effects of it. Yet a country that continues its old ignorance will retain its old religion. Thus barbarous nations, converted to Christianity, received the externals of the faith; but there they stopped. Only when the savage ignorance was removed, could the higher religion enter. Thus religion is an effect of man's improvement, not a cause of it. Intellectual activity must precede religious improvement. When Rome adopted Christianity, the barbarous empire, the barbarous Teutonic conquerors, were not ready for it: they substituted a Catholic polytheism for the pagan beliefs that had preceded it. There was no relief from this until European intellects roused from their lethargy. Only the Reformation ended the reign of such superstitions. Yet ignorant countries, upon which Protestantism happened to be fastened, remained as superstitious as Catholic countries which continued ignorant. Scotland, for instance, and Sweden, exhibit more bigotry, superstition, and intolerance, than Catholic France. The French have a religion worse than themselves; the Scotch, a religion better than themselves. The civilization does not proceed from the creed; normally, it produces the religion.

Literature, the second of these forces, is simply "the form in which the knowledge of the country is registered." From literary men we hear too much of the necessity of protecting and rewarding literature, and too little of the necessity for that freedom and boldness which alone gives worth to literature. Real knowledge consists solely in an acquaintance with physical and mental laws. Literature, being the depository of the thoughts of mankind, has absurdities as well as wisdom in it. Even an advanced culture shows a tendency to favor literature favoring ancient prejudices, rather than that opposing them. Thus the monks shuddered at the daring of the ancient writers, and substituted for it their own feeble and wretched superstitions. No literature can ever benefit a people, unless it finds them in a state of preliminary preparation.

Government, the third of these forces, is even less entitled to credit for creating civilization. Rulers are at best the creatures of an age, never its creators. Their measures are the result of social progress, not the cause of it. No great reform has ever been originated by rulers; bold and able thinkers have in every case first suggested it. Thus the abolition of English corn laws was caused, not by the wisdom of parliament, or the Anti-Corn-Law League; but by the march of public opinion, instigated by the reasoning of the political economists. Moreover, every great reform which has been effected has consisted, "not in doing something new, but in undoing something old. The most valuable additions made to legislation have been enactments destructive of preceding legislation; and the best laws which have been passed have been those by which some former laws were repealed." The only result was to place things on the same footing as if legislators had never interfered at all. The same is true of the decrease of religious persecutions: legislators have only retraced their own steps, and undone their own work. The whole tendency of modern legislation is "to restore things to that natural channel from which the ignorance of preceding legislation has driven them."

Indeed, the mischiefs governmental interference has caused have been so great, that the wonder is how civilization could advance with such repeated obstacles. Barring a few laws concerning the preservation of order and the punishment of crime, every English law has been an error. The affect of legislation to encourage trade has been to suppress it, and to ruin the traders. This was carried to the point where government robbed the industrious, on the pretense of aiding industry. Bad as the economic evils were, the moral ones were worse. Numerous and powerful gangs of armed smugglers sprang up, who lived by disobeying the laws which their ignorant rulers had imposed. These spread vice and crime broadcast—offenses caused by the laws. Now that the laws have been repealed, the offenses have ceased. The most that government can do, is to afford opportunity for progress; the progress itself must depend upon other matters.

"Seeing, therefore, that the efforts of government in favor of civilization are, when most successful, altogether negative; and seeing, too, that when those efforts are more than negative, they become injurious—it clearly follows that all speculations must be erroneous which ascribe the progress of Europe to the wisdom of its rulers." Every page of history supplies facts to support this opinion. Efforts to enforce religious belief had two leading consequences: to increase hypocrisy and perjury. The second is evidenced by the requirement of constant oaths, in the name of the Deity, from college boys to the highest officials in the land. This has become a source of national corruption, has diminished the worth of human testimony, and shaken the confidence which men naturally place in the word of their fellows. The governments have long sought to destroy the freedom of the press; they have taxed all channels of imparting information —a blackmail government extorts from literature, "to swell the pomp of an idle and ignorant court, minister to the caprice of a few powerful individuals, and too often supply them with the means of turning against the people resources which the people called into existence." The aggregate of all these is so formidable, that it is amazing that civilization has been able to advance.

CHAPTER III

ORIGIN OF HISTORY: HISTORY DURING THE MIDDLE AGES

LONG before a people are acquainted with the use of letters, they feel the want of some resource, which in peace may amuse their leisure, and in war may stimulate their courage. This is supplied to them by the invention of ballads, which form the groundwork of all historical knowledge, and which are found among many of the rudest tribes on earth. People without letters select the best form to assist their memory; "the first rudiments of knowledge consist always of poetry, and often of rhyme." These jingles rose ultimately to the dignity of judicial authorities, and the bards became the judges of disputed matters. The earliest ballads were approximately all strictly true; the singers were not likely to be mistaken on matters, in the accuracy of which they had so lively an interest.

The art of writing completely altered national traditions. It gave them permanence; and then weakened the traditions, weakened the class of bards, and encouraged falsehood. Various local heroes of the same name were each saddled with the exploits of the others; thus several truths were fused into an error. Thus a tribe of Finns called Quaens, occupying Quaenland on the Gulf of Bothnia, gave rise to stories of Amazons north of the Baltic. Thus, too, the ancient capital of Finland was called, in Swedish, Turku; which led sober historians to say that Turks inhabited Finland. The name Coeur de Lion similarly gave rise to the story that Richard had slain a lion. Moreover, when a knowledge of Christianity was communicated with the art of writing, the

28

monks falsified the national traditions, by blending them with monkish legends. The second Edda, a monkish compilation, is thus filled with Greek, Jewish, and Christian fables, including a widely diffused fiction of Trojan descent.

Wherever a change of religion has taken place, history is less trustworthy. India and China, where religions remained unchanged, possess traditions uncontaminated; Persia, conquered by the Mahometans, illustrates the opposite tendency. Malayo-Polynesian records, after the Mahometan conquest in the fifteenth century, show the same corruption; the traditions have gone, and even the Javanese lists of kings show interpolated Mahometan saints. On the neighboring island of Bali, where the old religion is still preserved, the legends of Java are remembered and cherished by the people. Similarly Christian priests obscured the annals of every European people they converted, including the Gauls, Welsh, Irish, Anglo-Saxons, Slavs, Finns, and Icelanders.

The literature of Europe, shortly before the Roman Empire fell, came into the hands of the clergy; and, monoplized by this single class, it assumed the peculiarities natural to its new masters. The business of the clergy was to enforce belief, not to encourage inquiry; hence, during many ages, literature injured society, by increasing credulity, and stopping the progress of knowledge. Thus the three leading causes of the corruption of the history of Europe, in the Middle Ages, were (1) the introduction of the art of writing, (2) the change of religion, and (3) clerical monopoly of the field. There was no history; its place was taken by falsehoods. Every people were taught that they were descended from ancestors present at the siege of Troy. The French, of course, must have come from Francus, son of Hector; the Britons from Brutus, whose father was Aeneas. Concerning origins of places, the historians of the Middle Ages were apparently informed of every incident since the moment Noah left the Ark, and, indeed, since Adam departed from Paradise. The capital of France was said to be named after Paris, son of Priam, who fled there when Troy was overthrown.

Tours owed its name to Turonus, a Trojan; Troyes clearly was settled by Trojans, as its name proved. Nuremberg was called after Nero, Jerusalem after the noted King Jebus, whom later historians have failed to locate. The river Humber was named from a Hunnish king who drowned in it; the Gauls, from Galathia, a female descendant of Japhet. Prussia was called after Prussus, brother to Augustus; Silesia, from the prophet Elisha, from whom the Silesians were told they were descended; Zurich was unquestionably built in the time of Abraham. The Scotch came from Egypt, named after Scota, daughter of Pharaoh.

Similarly, the city of Naples was founded on eggs; the order of St. Michael was instituted in person by that archangel, who originated chivalry, and was the first knight. The Tartars, of course, came from Tartarus, or hell. Since the Cross had fallen into Turkish hands, all Christian children had ten teeth less than formerly—apparently an irreparable calamity. Matthew Paris, the most eminent historian of the Middle Ages, explained that Mahometans refused to eat pork, because their prophet, drunk, had been smothered to death by a litter of pigs. Mahomet, of course, had originally been a cardinal, and had turned heretic when he failed in his design to become pope. Mathew of Westminster, a noted fourteenth century historian, ascertained that Judas slew his father, and married his mother. Pope Leo's hand, cut off to preserve the pope from sexual thrill when a woman had squeezed it, still existed in Rome, uncorrupted after five to six hundred years. The Lateran was named from "latente rana," Latin for hidden frog, a bloody frog vomited by Nero, believed to be the emperor's progeny, and buried by that emperor. Such were the notions taught in the ages of darkness, "or, as they have been well called, Ages of Faith."

The most popular histories were the stories of Arthur and Charlemagne, the latter written by Archbishop Turpin of Rheims, a friend of the emperor. The great conqueror, in this account, brought down the walls of Pamplona by prayer; Orlando, Charlemagne's knight, being worsted by the giant

Fenacute, twenty cubits high, as strong as forty men, vanquished the giant in a theological discussion, and then fatally wounded him. Geoffrey, Archdeacon of Monmouth, wrote the story of Arthur, with the aid of Walter, Archdeacon of Oxford. Brutus the Trojan, first settler of Britain, found the country overrun with giants, all of whom he slew; whereupon he built London. During the reign of King Rivallo, it rained blood for three consecutive days; a horrid sea monster, during the period of King Morvidus, ate innumerable people, and finally swallowed the king's self. Arthur at length entered upon the scene; slew countless Saxons, overran Norway, invaded Gaul, fixed his court at Paris, and prepared to conquer all Europe. He killed two giants in single combat, one who ate his prisoners alive, the other clothed in furs made of the beards of kings he had slain. Such was the history issued during the dark ages, written by high dignitaries of the church. The citations have been from the most celebrated histories of the period, and indicate fairly its trend.

The faults were not caused by deficiencies of the early historians; the average intellect of men is probably always the same; it is the pressure exerted on them by society which constantly alters. Later, when men like Machiavelli turned to history, they could do no more than use it as a vehicle for political speculations. Comines was a great observer; but instead of noting the oncoming intellectual revolution, he gave his pages to trivial intrigues. He blamed all political failures to interference by the Deity; for, says Comines, war is a great mystery, and being used by God as the means of accomplishing his wishes, he gives victory, sometimes to one side, sometimes to the other. Such attempts to make history a mere branch of theology are characteristic of the time, advocated, not by a monk in his cloister, but by a distinguished statesman, well versed in public affairs.

At first the Protestant Reformation was unfavorable to history, by encouraging able men in the discussion of questions inaccessible to human reason. The mood of the times is shown in the celebrated prediction, in 1524, by the astronomer Stoeffler, who reformed the Julian calendar, that the world would be destroyed that year by a second deluge. This prophecy caused lively and universal alarm; houses were abandoned; it was proposed that Emperor Charles V appoint inspectors to survey the probable points of safety in the land. An ecclesiastic named Auriol, professor of canon law at the University of Toulouse, at last suggested that an ark be built: and this was done. Seventy years later, it was reported that a child with a golden tooth had been born in Silesia. The miracle was soon known all over Germany. In 1595 the eminent physician, Dr. Horst, explained that, at the birth of the child, the sun was in conjunction with Saturn, at the sign Aries. The event was supernatural, but not alarming. The golden tooth was precursor of a golden age, in which the emperor would drive the Turks from Christendom, and found an empire to last thousands of years. As Horst pointed out, the prophet Daniel clearly forecast this, when he spoke of a statue with a golden head.

CHAPTER IV

Toleration in England.—This was the condition of the public mind, three hundred years ago. It is evident that, until doubt began, progress was impossible. Knowledge is not an inert and passive principle, which comes to us whether we will or no; it must be sought before it can be won. Those who do not feel the darkness, will never look for the light. The very names of doubt and scepticism are abominations to the ignorant, because they disturb lazily complacent minds, trouble cherished superstitions, and impose the fatigue of inquiry. The more we examine this great spirit of scepticism, the more distinctly shall we see the immense part it has played in the progress of European civilization. It has reformed every department of practical and speculative knowledge; it has weakened the authority of the privileged classes, and placed liberty on a surer basis; it has chastized princes, curbed the arrogance of nobles, and even lessened the prejudices of the clergy.

A careful study of religious toleration will prove, that in every Christian country where it has been adopted, it has been forced upon the clergy by the authority of the non-clerical classes. When Elizabeth mounted the throne, our country was balanced between two hostile creeds: and the queen so played off one against the other, that she gave the first instance in Europe of a nation carried on without the active participation of the clergy. When intolerance came into the end of her reign, no one was openly executed for religious opinion; as a subterfuge, political principles were said to be the cause of the executions. The fanatic had become a hypocrite—an advance from fanaticism.

33

A comparison between Hooker's "Ecclesiastical Polity" and Jewel's "Apology for the Church of England," written thirty years before, shows the change. The authors were men of equal genius and learning; both wrote to defend the Church of England. The thirty years elapsing before 1594, when Hooker's work appeared, had been marked by a great progress in the English intellect. Jewel accepted quotations from the Fathers and the Councils as unanswerable arguments; Hooker slights the Fathers, and indicates that his readers would be more moved by reason than authority. Jewel inculcates the importance of faith; Hooker insists upon the exercise of reason. Living in the age of Shakespeare and Bacon, he appealed not to tradition, commentators, nor revelation, but held that the needs of society would be the final test.

Once let the old dogmatic method give way to human reasoning, and the element of uncertainty had been let in. From this moment, persecution became a crime of the deepest dye. As theology became more reasonable, it became less confident, and therefore more merciful. Scepticism in physics must be the beginning of science; in religion, of toleration. After this, a general spirit of inquiry, of doubt, of insubordination, began to fill the minds of men. In physics, this enabled men to overthrow the shackles of superstition, and beget science. In politics, it stirred them to rise against the government, and behead their king. In religion, it vented itself in a thousand sects, many exaggerating the limits of private judgment. Chillingworth's "Religion of Protestants," appearing in 1637, marks the completion of the change. All authority in matters of religion is openly set at defiance. Chillingworth would admit no reservation tending to limit the sacred right of private judgment. He asks if religious doctrines are in accord with human reason; he does not hesitate to say that no man is bound to believe anything repugnant to his own understanding. Faith is not supreme; reason gives us knowledge, he says, while faith gives only belief, a part of knowledge, and therefore inferior to it.

This immense work justified the breaking-up of the

Anglican church, which the same generation lived to witness. If the ultimate test of truth is individual judgment, and man's judgments are fallible, it follows that there is no decisive standard of religious truth. "This is a melancholy, and, as I firmly believe, a most inaccurate conclusion;" but it is necessary, before man can achieve that toleration that is the final attitude. Ultimately will come religion by that purely transcendental process, of which glimpses in every age have been granted to a few gifted minds. But scepticism is necessary, to destroy effectually religious fanaticism.

During the 17th century, scepticism and toleration advanced together; though the two successors of Elizabeth did all they could to reverse her enlightened policy. During the reigns of James and Charles, theology was for the first time merged into politics. It was no longer a struggle of creeds and dogmas; it was a struggle between those who favored the crown, and those who supported the parliament. The violent death of the king ultimately strengthened the power of the crown; but it harmed the church. England was ruled by men who called themselves Independents; who beat back the pretensions of the clergy, and professed unbounded contempt for clerical rites and dogmas. It is noteworthy, too, that the Puritans were more fanatical than superstitious. "They were so ignorant of the real principles of government as to direct penal laws against private vices; and to suppose that immorality could be stemmed by legislation." But they resisted the aggressions even of their own clergy; and after the Restoration, religion, though restored in ancient pomp, had lost its ancient power. The new king, from levity, rather than reason, despised the disputes of theologians, and treated religion with indifference; his courtiers followed his example. The latter attempted to fortify their doubts by the blasphemous expression of a wild and desperate infidelity. They were the unwholesome offspring of that spirit of disbelief which characterized the Englishman of the 17th century. It was this which caused Locke to be an innovator in philosophy, a Unitarian in creed; which made Newton a Socinian, and Milton an enemy of the church, and perhaps an Arian in *Paradise Lost*.

The progress against superstition was aided by the zeal shown in the physical sciences. In 1633, Sir Thomas Browne wrote his credulous *Religio Medici;* in 1646, appeared the same writer's *Inquiries into Vulgar and Common Errors.* This was the first systematic and deliberate onslaught made in England upon superstition. The twelve years between the two works had completed that vast social and intellectual revolution of which the overthrow of the church and the beheading of the king were but minor incidents. Instead of the credulity of the former book, we have now "the two great pillars of truth, experience and solid reason." Adherence unto authority, neglect of inquiry, and credulity are given as main causes of error. With such rapidity did England move. At this time appeared the physicist Boyle, who insisted in his great researches upon individual experiments, and upon the unimportance of facts handed down from antiquity. At this same time the Royal Society was incorporated by Charles II, its object to extend natural knowledge as opposed to supernatural.

Nearly all the clergy allied themselves against science. Sailors and agriculturists naturally ascribe happenings to supernatural interference; soldiers and manufacturers are inclined to be less superstitious. Even today (1855, also 1926) we see prayers offered up in our churches for dry weather or for wet weather; we are not ashamed, in our public churches, "to prostitute the rites of religion by using them as a cloak to conceal an ignorance we ought frankly to confess." In spite of the political and moral confusion and weakness in the government, this reign forms a bright epoch in English history. For this age saw a law, which took from bishops the right to burn those who disagree with them; the clergy were deprived of the right to tax themselves; the church was deprived of the right to make a criminal incriminate himself; the House of Lords was deprived of original jurisdiction in civil suits; all taxation must be by the people's representatives; the Habeas Corpus Act made a man's liberty comparatively safe; the liberty of printing was safeguarded; the Norman feudal impositions were ended; and other important reforms achieved. All this was done, in spite of the criminal incompetency of the king, in spite of the great plague, the great fire. All this was done because history is not the result of the personal peculiarities of rulers, but of the intellectual development of the people. These reforms proceeded from that bold, sceptical, and inquiring spirit, which now held theology, science and politics.

Charles led the way in despising the clergy openly. Hobbes, subtlest dialectician of his time, was the most dangerous opponent of the superstitious class—and the king treated him with a scandalous respect. When it came to ecclesiastical appointments, the king chose men noted for their weakness of intellect and influence. Jeremy Taylor and Isaac Barrow, the two outstanding clerics of ability, were uniformly slighted; even though Taylor was married to the king's bastard sister. The accession of Catholic James II, at this time, resulted fortunately. The Anglican forces at first conspired with the king in many cruelties; and only split with him when he issued his Declaration of Indulgences, an edict of toleration. As long as the king's victims were opponents of the English Church, the churchmen observed his revolting cruelties with sanctimonious complacency. The moment James turned to protect against persecution those hostile to the Church, almost to a man the churchmen revolted, and refused to read in their churches the declaration of toleration. In desperation, they turned for aid against the king to the very dissenters they had been persecuting. This union, inspired by the edict of toleration, cost the king his crown. It should never be forgotten that the first and only time the Church of England made war against the crown was when the crown exhibited religious toleration.

The Revolution of 1688.—It is difficult to conceive the full impetus given to English civilization by the expulsion of the Stuarts. This included the limitations upon royal power, steps toward religious toleration, an improved administration of justice, abolition of censorship over the press, and the growth of the great monetary class. All this came in the reign of William III. No sooner had the new prince come in, than the Church of England repented of its step. The last days of James had been marked by increasing friendliness to Anglican interests; so much so, that the majority of them turned against the great prince they had invited in as ruler. The Archbishop of Canterbury rebuked his chaplain for praying for the new rulers; he refused the oath of allegiance, as did the Bishops of Bath and Wells, of Chester, of Chichester, of Ely, of Gloucester, of Norwich, of Peterborough, and of Worcester. Six hundred of the lesser clergy aped their elders and betters. This made the issue clear, between the clergy on one side, and, on the other, the intellect of England, and all her dearest interests.

Such a course of action only harmed the clergy. When the bishops refused to take the oath, William ejected by force the Archbishop of Canterbury and five of his colleagues. The clergy hysterically denied the right of king or legislature to restrain them; and, collaborating with banished James, they continued a rival succession of imaginary bishops which lasted until 1779, or more than a century. Others of the clergy made the fine mental distinction between a king by right and a king in possession; taking a lip oath to William, and paying heart homage to James. This made concealed rebels of a large body of the clergy; and the open lies of the clergy aided further the growth of the general spirit of scepticism. The Convocation, or meeting of the clergy in a body, began to lose power; in 1717, this celebrated assembly was dismissed by the king, since the nation had no further need of it.

The tendency of affairs became notorious. Able men no longer flocked into the church, but preferred those secular professions where ability stood a higher chance of being rewarded. Since the 17th century, there has been no instance of any churchman being made Lord Chancellor; since the beginning of the 18th century, none have served in any important role in diplomatic or governmental circles. In the barbarous beginning of English history, one half of the House of Lords were bishops; by the middle of the 19th century, their number has shrunk to one-fourteenth. More than fifty years has elapsed since a clergyman has been able to take his seat in the lower house, as a representative of the people; in 1801 the door of the Commons was formally closed against the clerics.

The dissenters had by no means forgotten the sixty thousand of their number punished between 1660 and 1688, and the five thousand of these who had died in prison; and now the political revolution was supplemented by a great religious revolution. After William III, foolish and ignorant Anne succeeded to the throne, and resumed persecution of the dissenters. After her death, the inevitable reaction came. Laws against dissenters were repealed; and two of the greatest men of the 18th century, Whitefield, the theological orator, and Wesley, the theological statesman, organized their great challenging system of religion. It is true that, since the death of their great leaders, the Wesleyans have produced not one man of original genius, nor a single scholar of European reputation; but this was due less to any fault in the sect than to the general decline of the theological spirit. Their injury to the Anglican body was enormous; the mere existence of a great rival sect, unopposed by the government, was a precedent full of promise for society. Theology became separated both from morals and from politics. Cumberland, bishop of Peterborough, first endeavored to construct a system of morals without the aid of theology; Warburton, bishop of Gloucester, first laid down that the state must consider religion in reference, not to revelation, but to expediency. His point was that a state should favor a creed, not because of its truth, but because of its general utility. The idea spread rapidly; and theology was finally divorced from both ethics and government.

This idea at first was confined to the intellectual classes, and did not at once reach practical form. Meanwhile, theological bickerings further weakened the church—disputes upon such matters as the confessional, miracles, the Heavenly

Witness, and other ecclesiastical fungi. This was accompanied by the discoveries of the geologists, which not only attacked the history of creation as narrated in Genesis, but showed that the Mosaic chronology was absurdly impossible. The changes began to reach the people. The increase of scepticism stimulated their curiosity; the diffusion of education supplied the means of gratifying it. It was at this time (1765) that there were first established schools for the lower classes, on Sunday, the only day they had time to attend them; and newspapers on Sunday, the only day they had time to read them. For the first time circulating libraries were seen in England; the art of printing spread from London to the country towns. Attempts were made to popularize the sciences by writing books upon them in an easy, untechnical style. Periodical literary reviews sprang up, containing information available for large bodies of practical men. Societies were formed to purchase books, and clubs were instituted by reading men among the industrious classes. By 1750, debating societies sprang up among tradesmen; in 1769 occurred a bolder innovation, the first public meeting ever assembled in England, in which it was attempted to enlighten Englishmen concerning their rights. The people began to study proceedings in the courts of law; political newspapers arose. At once there was sharp conflict between them and the House of Lords, concerning the right to publish the debates; and, in the end, both houses, aided by the crown, were entirely defeated.

On the heel of this came the promulgation of the great doctrine of personal representation in politics. All of these forces altered literature from its early style of powerful, cumbrous, involved sentences into a lighter and simpler style. Literature in general began to be addressed to the common miscellaneous public. These factors gave greater independence to literary men, and greater boldness in literary inquiries. The patronage of the rich, the noble, the royal, was succeeded by popular patronage: "Those servile and shameful dedications; that mean and crouching spirit; that incessant

homage to mere rank and birth; that constant confusion between power and right; that ignorant admiration for everything which is old, and that still more ignorant contempt
for everything which is new—all these features became gradually fainter." The issue of the great disputes now became
commonly known to the people, as never before.

The Hanoverians.—Unfortunate political combinations succeeded, which, among any other people, would have ended
either in a loss of liberty or in a dissolution of government.
After the death of Anne, two princes succeeded, alien in manners and in country, one of whom spoke the language only
passably, and the other not at all. They were unable to do
anything to extend royal power; and thus the nation was
secure in the progress of its spirit of inquiry. The old Tory
faction, pressed by the people, and abandoned by the crown,
was unable for more than forty years to take any share in
the government.

Then George III came in—a king born in England, who
spoke English as his mother tongue, and looked upon Hanover
as a foreign country. At the same time, the Stuart pretender was languishing in Italy, where he soon afterwards
died; and his son, abject and stupid, was consuming his life
in an unpitied and despicable obscurity, as a drunkard in
Rome. It was George III who suddenly revived those monstrous doctrines regarding the rights of kings, which the
Revolution of 1688 was supposed to have destroyed. The
clergy abandoned the hopeless pretender, and flocked over
zealously to the Hanoverian. The old Tory faction rapidly
rallied, and soon dispossessed their rivals in control of the
government. George III, "without knowledge, without taste,
without even a glimpse of one of the sciences, or a feeling for
one of the fine arts," had a puny mind which education had
not aided. Totally ignorant of the history and resources of
foreign countries, barely knowing their geographical position,
he knew no more about the people whom he was ruling.

Such a ruler gathered around the throne that great party
which enshrined the traditions of the past, and made it their

boast to check the progress of the age. During his reign of sixty years, he never admitted to his·councils a man of ability, with the sole exception of Pitt. Pitt maintained his place by forgetting the lessons of his great father, and abandoning those liberal principles he professed on entering public life Pitt did not even hesitate to persecute to the death the party he had formerly been allied with. George III looked upon slavery as one of the good old customs; hence Pitt did not dare touch it. George III detested the French; Pitt therefore engaged in a perilous war, which saddled upon England a debt which can never be paid off. When Pitt toward the end showed a disposition to concede to the Irish some small share of their undoubted rights, the king dismissed him peremptorily from office. He was reinstated only upon his agreeing to surrender his principle in this matter.

No other man of ability was called on to aid. Fox, talented and serene in temper, was barred by George III from the list of privy councillors, the king declaring angrily that he would abdicate before admitting Fox to a share in the government. Up to this time, the Lords had been superior to the Commons, the latter consisting of mere fox-hunting squires, leaning toward the Tory side. The Lords protected Somers and Walpole from persecution by the Commons; they stood against the Schism act, intended to permit persecution of dissenters. But George III filled up the peers with nonentities, rich ignorant country gentlemen and reactionary lawyers; no great thinkers, writers, orators, or statesmen were appointed by him. None of the intelligent banking and commercial classes were named beside the spurious nobles the king created. Political degeneracy, thus indicated, appeared on every side.

A signal exception was Edmund Burke, philosophical lawyer, and student of the fine arts, acquainted also with physics and even the routine of mechanical trades. His political principles were always practical; his motto was that the aim of the legislator should be, not truth, but expediency. He made his individual opinions subservient to the march of events, regarding the happiness of the people at large as the thing to strive for; the happiness to be determined by their wishes, not his ideas. He advocated free trade, supported the dissenters, favored the harassed debtors; he reformed finances, and nobly supported the American colonists on the ground of the inexpediency of harassing them. Yet for thirty years such a man received neither favor nor reward from the crown: this most eminent of English politicians was totally neglected. Toward his death, Burke fell into a state of complete hallucination. The excesses of the French Revolution unbalanced his reason. The intense bereavement caused by the death of his only son increased his mental perturbation and his last phase was one of insane hatred of all things connected with the French Revolution. He broke with Fox, he insulted other friends, who dared to support France's right to conduct its own affairs in its own way. This extended to such Frenchmen as Lafayette and Condorcet: the distinguished latter of whom Burke called a "fanatic atheist," and the former of whom he called a "horrid ruffian." France he called "Cannibal Castle," a nation of murderous atheists, robbers, plunderers, the scum of the earth. He plagued for a war against France: "I speak it emphatically, and with a desire that it should be marked, I desire a *long* war." The war was to be for revenge as well as defense; to force men to change their government, to alter their religion. Only a diseased mind could have uttered this: and this lowered him to the level of the royal intellect. Now it was that George III gave him two extensive pensions, and wished to raise the unbalanced dotard to the peerage.

During the reign of George II, it was proposed to increase royal revenues by taxing the unrepresented colonies—a scheme of public robbery at once rejected. Under George III, this policy was at once put into force. The clergy, the aristocracy, sided with the ruler: and a war ensued, "ill-conducted, unsuccessful, and, what is far worse, accompanied by cruelties disgraceful to a civilized nation." Among the expenses of the war which the government laid before parliament was an item for "five gross of scalping knives." Victory over America would have overturned the liberties of Englishmen at home. Heroically the Americans prevented this. England then turned against France, withdrawing its ambassador when the French did away with their monarchy, and substituted a republic in its place. When France beheaded its king, as England had done less than two centuries before, England at once ordered every Frenchman in England to quit the country; thus originating a war which lasted twenty years, cost the lives of millions, and stopped the march of civilization, by postponing for a generation imminent reforms.

The duty of the English government now became twofold: to destroy a republic abroad, and prevent improvement at home. The latter it endeavored to do, by laws intended to suppress free discussion of political questions, and stifle the spirit of inquiry. More than a score of prominent English liberals were persecuted and punished, imprisoned or transported, for expressing their sentiments with freedom. In 1795, public meetings were forbidden if a single magistrate ordered it. If the meeting consisted of twelve or more, and these remained for an hour after being ordered to disperse, the penalty was death. Circulating libraries and reading rooms were next attacked; lending books without permission of a magistrate was punishable by a fine, and the lender was guilty of keeping a disorderly house. Fox retorted that resistance to such a government was merely a matter of prudence: yet the government continued in its headlong career. The ministers filled the jails with their political opponents; every popular leader was in personal danger; every popular assemblage was dispersed. Habeas corpus was suspended; the crown could imprison without inquiry. Taxes were laid on nearly every product of industry and nature, to support the oppression of popular liberties.

On the surface, this pointed to a despotic government. But underneath all this was the progressive intellectual movement. The increase and diffusion of knowledge, in England, was antagonistic to all these political events. The political oppressions accordingly were all in vain; in a few years, the system of tyranny fell to the ground. The vigor of an arbitrary government depends merely on a few individuals, who are liable, after death, to be replaced by weaklings; the vigor of public opinion is not liable to such a casualty. The great change was effected, not by external event, or sudden insurrection, but by the unaided action of moral force—the silent, though overwhelming, pressure of public opinion. This indicates the healthy march of English civilization. The English people were wise enough to stay their hand, to husband their force until they could use it with irresistible effect. For fifty years the movement has proceeded with unimpeded vigor. The Reform Bill, the emancipation of the Catholics, the repeal of the Corn Laws, the extension of the suffrage, the abolition of protection, these and other steps marked the steady upward march of popular rights.

This was brought about by destroying the evil system of George III, rather than by improving the men. The system perished because it was unsuited to the age; a progressive people will never tolerate an unprogressive government. This should moderate the presumption of legislators, and teach them "that their best measures are but temporary expedients, which it will be the business of a later and riper age to efface." Politics is still, not a science, but a backward art; the only safe course for the legislator is, to look upon his craft as "the adaptation of temporary contrivances to temporary emergencies." His business is to follow the age, not to attempt to lead it.

CHAPTER V

Scepticism and Toleration in France.—The best way of arriving at a theory of disease is by beginning with a theory of health. Similarly great social truths can best be studied in a society which has developed itself according to its own laws, with the least opposition from the governing powers. Thus, to understand the position of France, this study has first considered the position of England. In France, a long train of events from an early period gave to the clergy a larger power than they possessed in England. At first this benefited, since the church restrained the lawlessness of a barbarous age. As the French advanced in knowledge, the spiritual authority began to press heavily upon their genius, and impede its movements. When the Reformation broke out, the weakened English church gave way to permit social progress: in France, the powerful clergy were able to withstand the Reformation, and thus retain the privileges which were used to restrain social progress.

Protestantism, far from being an aberration arising from accidental causes, was essentially a normal movement, a legitimate expression of the wants of the European intellect. The Reformation owed its success, not to a desire to purify the church, but to a desire to lighten its burdens. It was adopted everywhere except where preceding events had made the clergy too powerful to be overthrown. Unhappily, this was the case in France; and this fact gave everything a more theological aspect in France than in England. By the 17th century, the English had produced a lasting literature, as one result of this liberated spirit; by that time the French had not produced a single work of lasting merit. This is one of the innumerable instances which "teach us that no country can rise to eminence so long as the ecclesiastical power possesses much authority."

Excesses of this theological aspect of France were shown in the conspiracy of Amboise, and in the conference of Poissy; and in those revolting crimes so natural to superstition, the massacres of Vassy and of St. Bartholomew, the murder of Guise by Poltrot, and of Henry III by Clément. These were legitimate fruits of bigotry. In 1589, however, Henry IV ascended the French throne—a great prince, who made small account of theological disputes, in contrast to his predecessors. Francis I had said that, if his right hand were a heretic, he would cut it off. Henry II declared he would "make the extirpation of heretics his principal business." Charles IX attempted to end the heretics by a single blow, the massacre of St. Bartholomew. Henry III promised to oppose heresy at the risk of his life. The powerful intellect of Henry IV had no sympathy with such narrow views. To suit the shifting policies of his age, he changed his religion thrice, and meditated a fourth switch. Only five years after he abjured Protestantism, he published the celebrated Edict of Nantes, by which a Catholic government for the first time granted to heretics a fair share of civil and religious rights. It was no royal act merely, but a part of a vast movement in which the people themselves participated; it was an expression of a rising spirit of scepticism among the people.

Rabelais has been called the first French sceptic; yet his writings do not earn that accolade. He treats the clergy with disrespect and ridicule; but only for their personal vices, not for the narrow spirit which caused the vices. But the extension of experience, and the consequent increase of knowledge, were preparing the way for a great change in the French intellect. A few years before the promulgation of the Edict of Nantes, appeared the first systematic sceptic who wrote in French. The Essays of Montaigne were published in 1588, and dated an epoch in the civilization of France. The difference between Rabelais and Montaigne is the difference between Jewel and Hooker, the difference between Hooker and Chillingworth. The writings of Montaigne were directed against the whole clerical system. They exhibited a spirit of lofty and audacious inquiry, masked under the nonchalance of a man of the world. His eminent readability made him popular, and prepared the way for Charron's celebrated *Treatise on Wisdom,* (1601), the first attempt made in a modern language to construct a system of morals without theology. The flippancy of Montaigne was here succeeded by a high gravity. He reminds his countrymen that their religion is an accident of birth and geography; born in a Moslem country, they could have been Moslems. Moreover, each religion, declaring itself to be the true one, is built on some earlier religion. We should discard the pretensions of all hostile sects, and be content with such practical religion as consists in performing the duties of life.

After this time, scepticism increased and fanaticism declined throughout the people. The clergy sought to have the government check the spirit of inquiry; the pope formally urged Henry to end the evil. Henry shrewdly leaned toward the weaker sect, the Protestants, to keep the powers equal; banished the Jesuits, gave money to the Protestants, and watched closely for infractions of their rights. On the murder of Henry IV in 1610, the queen administered the power during the infancy of her son Louis XIII. She, although a weak and bigoted woman, refrained from religious persecutions—another evidence of the power of the spirit of popular scepticism. She sustained the Edict of Nantes; and, in 1614, when her son attained his majority, his first act was to confirm the same expression of toleration. At this time Richelieu took over the reins of government, a control he held during the last eighteen years of the reign of Louis XIII. He differed from Napoleon, in that the later conqueror was a constant oppresser of man's liberties; Richelieu was the contrary. His attempts to limit the power of the nobles broke down at his death, and the nobles quickly rallied. Yet even such an attempt, from a bishop and cardinal, was astonishing. Priest as he was, he made no effort to increase the power of the priestly class. He broke the power of royal confessors over matters of state, required clerical financial support of government projects, and exiled four bishops and two archbishops who opposed him.

The indignation of the clergy against such a recreant cleric burst forth in full vehemence. They scattered odious libels against him: that he was unchaste, guilty of open debauchery, that he practiced incest with his niece; that he was pontiff of the Huguenots, patriarch of atheists. Richelieu persisted, openly repudiating the pernicious doctrine that it was a duty of government to suppress heresy. At home and abroad he aided the Protestants, giving support to German Lutherans, Dutch Protestants, and others whom the church called rebellious heretics. He made what Sismondi fairly calls a "Protestant confederation" with England and Holland. Two years after his death, the Congress of Westphalia concluded that peace which altogether disregarded churchly interests, and indeed seized church property to recompense lay governments —a blow from which the spiritual power never recovered. The Thirty Years War, which this peace ended, was the last great religious war ever waged.

Richelieu elevated many Protestants, Rohan, Lesdiguières, Chatillon, La Force, and others, to the military leadership of the army. Such steps encouraged men to look to their country as the first consideration; discarding old disputes, Catholic soldiers were taught to obey heretic generals, and follow their standards to victory. This social amalgamation in the camps aided the general increase of scepticism.

Protestant Intolerance.—Yet, while the prejudices of the Catholics obviously diminished, those of the Protestants for a time retained their activity. It is a striking proof of the perversity of such feelings, that it was in that country, and that period, when the Protestants were best treated, that they displayed most turbulence. Toleration had weaned the noble

Protestant leaders into the Catholic fold; not as earnest believers, but as indifferent sceptics, who took the name of the older, more established faith for motives of expediency. The Dukes de Lesdiguières, de la Trémouille, de la Meilleraye, de Bouillon, and the Marquis de Montausier, took this course. The Maréchal de Bouillon, the Duke de Sully, the Marquis de Chatillon, did not alter allegiance, but displayed complete indifference to religion in their actions. This movement threw the management of the French Protestant party into the hands of the clergy: and this body, here as everywhere, was noted for its intolerance.

This instance shows how superficial is the opinion of those writers, who hold that the Protestant religion is necessarily more liberal than the Catholic. The Protestant religion is, for the most part, more tolerant than the Catholic, because the events which have given rise to Protestantism have at the same time increased the play of the intellect. But the desire to burn their opponents burned as hot in the great Calvinist divines as in the Catholics; there is now more superstition, more bigotry, among the lower Scotch Presbyterians, than among the lower order of French Catholics. The actions of men are governed, not by dogmas and text-books, but by the opinions and habits of their contemporaries, and by the general spirit of the age. As the interest of the clergy waned among the French Catholics, it increased among their Protestants. A religion not protected by the government usually displays greater energy and vitality than a protected one. The theological spirit first weakens in the educated classes: and when they surrender the leadership of a movement to the clergy, intolerance is likely to creep in, as among the French Protestants. The situation of the Irish Catholics today parallels the French Protestant situation then.

Thus, under such leadership, French Protestants soon grew to despise that great Edict of Nantes, by which their liberties were secured. They were not content to exercise their own religion, unless they could trouble the religion of others. They held a great assembly at Saumur, shortly after the death of

Henry IV, and formally demanded an end to the ancient Catholic processions in towns and places occupied now by Protestants. When the government showed no disposition toward this intolerance, the Protestants took the law into their own hands. They attacked Catholic processions, insulted Catholic priests, and even endeavored to prevent them from administering the sacrament to the sick, or burying the dead. At La Rochelle, second city in the kingdom, they forbade the Catholics from having a single church. They forbade intermarriages between the faiths, and withheld the sacrament from the parents whose children married into Catholic families. When Louis XIII, in 1620, visited Pau, he was not only treated with indignity, as a heretical prince, but he found that the Protestants had left not a single church where the King of France, in his own territory, could perform his own and the recognized religion.

Those who left Protestantism for Catholicism were insulted by the Protestant clergy in the grossest manner, with every term of abuse. In 1613 a Protestant, Ferrier, was excommunicated for speaking slightingly of churchly assemblies, and was "delivered up unto Satan." The inflamed people rose against Ferrier, attacked his family, destroyed his property, sacked and gutted his houses, demanded that the "traitor Judas" be given to them. Minority as they were, the Protestants sought to control the crown; and endeavored to dictate what wife the king should wed. With a view of exasperating further religious hatreds, the Protestant clergy put forth a series of works, which for bitterness of feeling have never been surpassed. They took over Catholic property to support their own churches; so the Protestant religion, permitted in part of the kingdom, in other parts refused to let the Catholics perform their own religion. The government interfered, and a brief rebellion occurred at Pau, which was soon put down. But the sword had been drawn: and the sword must now decide whether France should be governed by toleration, or according to the maxims of a despotic Protestant sect.

Scarcely was the war in Bearn ended, when the Protestants

determined on a great effort in Rochelle, in the west of France. This strong fortress was entirely in the hands of Protestants; and here, in December 1620, their spiritual chiefs flocked from all France, bent on violent measures. Their first act confiscated all Catholic property; they caused a great seal to be struck, and taxes to be collected to defend their religion. They organized their establishment, the Reformed Churches of France and Bearn, parcelling out France into eight circles alloted to eight generals, accompanied by eight clergymen. The war that broke out lasted seven years, and was uninterrupted, except by the brief peaces of Montpelier and Rochelle. The Protestants sought religious domination; the Catholics, temporal advantages. Thus the secular principle was represented by the Catholics, the theological one by the Protestants. If the Protestants had carried the day, this victory of ecclesiastical bigotry would have been an enormous loss to France. Clerical tyrants trouble men in their most ordinary pursuits, in their amusements, even in the dress they are to wear, all in the name of virtue! The French Protestants forbade any one to go to the theatre, or dance, while dancing masters who persisted in this iniquity were to be excommunicated. Gay apparel was prohibited, and hair must be worn soberly; women were forbidden to paint; Greek must not be taught, it being a non-sacred language. Chemistry was likewise forbidden: nothing could be published without church sanction; balls and masquerades, conjuring tricks, morris dances, were to be strictly avoided. Children's names should be taken from the Bible, but should not be Baptist, Angel, or any name pagans had used; hair should be cut short, dresses could not have tassels, gloves must be shorn of silk and ribands; "fardingales and wide sleeves" must be excommunicated.

The Protestants were the more aggressive party; but, fortunately for France, only three years after the war began, in 1624, Richelieu assumed the direction of the government. His own clergy urged him to exterminate the Protestant heretics: he strove for tolerance. He determined to chastise the rebellion, but not punish the heresy. He determined on a decisive siege of Rochelle; and, in 1628, took the place. His victory was marked by toleration; but, in a year, in another part of France, the Protestants rose again. They were now easily defeated; but again toleration was extended to them.

Thus Richelieu secularized French politics; and at the same time, the profoundest thinker France ever produced was engaged in a similar course in a still higher department. This was René Descartes, who effected "a revolution more decisive than has ever been brought about by any other single mind." On the physical field, he first applied algebra to geometry; pointed out the law of the sines; discovered the changes to which light is subjected in the eye by the crystalline lens; pointed out the consequences of the weight of the atmosphere; detected the causes of the rainbow; and performed laborious experiments upon the animal frame. More than these, he is the author of what is emphatically called modern philosophy. Great as creator, he was greater as a destroyer. His *Method* is essentially and exclusively psychological. He sought truth by plucking out all old opinions, directing his scepticism, not against the human intellect, but against authority and tradition. Nothing, says Descartes, is certain but thought; the man himself is the thought. From this we rise to a perception of the Deity. "For, our belief in his existence is an irrefragable proof that he exists. Otherwise whence does this belief arise? Since nothing can come out of nothing, and since no effect can be without a cause, it follows that the idea we have of God must have an origin; and this origin, whatever name we give it, is no other than God." Such a philosophy was fatal to common dogmas like transubstantiation, and to authority in general. But both Richelieu and Descartes succeeded not only because of their abilities, but because of the general temper of the times. The nature of their labors depended upon themselves; the way in which their labors were received, upon their contemporaries.

A few months after the death of Richelieu, Louis XIII also died, and the crown passed to Louis XIV, a child. During his minority, Mazarin held the power—a man inferior to Richelieu, but animated by the latter's spirit. His first act was to confirm the Edict of Nantes. During the twenty years of his control, no Frenchman was punished for his religion. Mazarin concluded an intimate alliance with the heretic Cromwell. During his control broke out the Fronde, that civil war in which the people sought to carry into politics the movement that had succeeded in literature and religion. Thus was the first contest in France by human beings for avowedly human purposes; a war waged by men, not to enforce their opinions, but to increase their liberty.

During this period, the English mind preceded the French, in similar activities, by nearly a whole generation. This must be due to the priority of the English antecedents, in each case. It is clear that the French knew less, because they believed more. In both countries, civil wars broke out at nearly the same time; in both the insurgents, successful at first, were afterwards defeated. The restorations, England in 1660, France in 1661, were almost simultaneous. But there the similarity stopped. England experienced thereafter a consolidation of national prosperity; France, a revolution more bloody and destructive than any the world had seen. Our inquiry is to ascertain why the French, who had hitherto paralleled the English progress, stopped short in their politics, fell under the despotism of Louis XIV, and never even cared to resist it. The cause of this difference is to be sought in the existence of that spirit of protection, that forms the chief obstacle which advancing civilization has to face. It has caused France's love of centralization, their protection in industry, their paternal government. Let us trace this spirit in France.

CHAPTER VI

History of the Protective Spirit: France and England.—
During the earlier dark ages, the clergy controlled reasoning,
and were friendly with it. Their attitude changed when the
advocates of inquiry began to challenge the advocates of belief.
This is the great starting-point of modern civilization. Just
at this period sprang up the feudal system. An inevitable
struggle commenced between feudality and the church. The
feudal system did not destroy the spirit of protection, but
expressed it in a new form; instead of being spiritual, it became temporal. Men, instead of looking up to the church,
looked up to the nobles. A hereditary aristocracy sprang up:
in the 10th century the first surnames, in the 11th offices
becoming hereditary, in the 12th the invention of armorial
bearings and heraldic devices came in, all nourishing the
conceit of nobles, and marking that superiority of birth which
so long was regarded as the primary superiority.

In the organization of society, feudality succeeded the
church; the hereditary nobles gradually displaced in government the clergy, who had adopted celibacy. An inquiry into
the protective spirit then involves an inquiry into the origin
of the aristocratic power, the cover under which the spirit
displayed itself. Soon after the middle of the 11th century,
while the aristocracy was still in process of formation, England was conquered by the Duke of Normandy, who brought
with him the beginnings of feudalism. But he was able to
dispense with certain French feudal usages. The great Norman lords, strangers amid a hostile population, were glad to
accept estates from the crown on almost any terms that

would guarantee their own security. This prevented the barons from possessing that power they had in France, and made them amenable to the law, or, at least, to the king. William, shortly before his death, made the landowners render their fealty to him; thus avoiding that peculiarity of feudalism, by which each vassal was separately dependent on his lord.

In France events proceeded differently. Nobles held their land, not by royal grant, but by prescription. The antiquity of this, added to the crown's weakness, made them independent sovereigns on their own estates. They could coin money, and wage private war: both rights were recognized by Louis IX and Philip the Fair, two kings of considerable energy. In England, the weakness of the nobles made them ally themselves with the people. Magna Charta came from such a coalition; the House of Commons owes its origin, in 1264, to a similar union. This gave the people that tone of independence to which civil and political institutions are the consequence, rather than the cause. The French lords did not need the aid of the people: hence society was divided into two classes, upper and lower, protectors and protected. Under the feudal system in France, every man was either a tyrant or a slave; or, by the process called subinfeudation, a combination of both. By subinfeudation, great lords granted lands to lesser lords, these to lesser holders, and so on down in an endless chain; thus organizing submission into a system.

When feudalism decayed, in the 14th century, the results of this difference were apparent. Englishmen, in some degree accustomed to self-government, held fast to their municipal rights, and their rights as yeomen. France knew no such rights; and, while charters were granted to the towns, and privileges ceded to the magistrates, all this was useless. The parchments of lawyers cannot preserve man's independence; liberty can only be retained by those accustomed to think and act for themselves. In France, under Louis XIV and Napoleon, this process was pushed to its limit. Everything must be referred to one common center, in which all civic functions were absorbed. All important local improvements, all schemes for bettering the condition of the people, must receive the sanction of government. To prevent magistrates from abusing their power, no power was conferred upon them. The government is believed to see everything, know everything, provide for everything. To enforce this monstrous monopoly, an immense array of machinery webs the country. The business of state is conducted on the supposition that no man knows his own interest, or is fit to take care of himself. To prevent improper bequests, the law prevents men from bequeathing the greater part of their property. Passports are required for travelling; the interfering spirit shackles every liberty of motion. In criminal trials, the judge is magistrate and prosecutor. Soldiers are present at all places of amusement; education is superintended by the state. Its prying eye follows the butcher to the shambles, and the baker to the oven.

The French have been found unfit to exercise political power. When they have had it, they have never been able to combine permanence with liberty. When the crown grew stronger, in the 14th century, the nobles grew weaker; but the subservience of the people to the nobles remained the same. In England, slavery, or villenage, as it was mildly termed, was gone by the end of the 16th century; in France, it lasted for two hundred years longer, and only went down in the red flood of the Revolution.

In the 11th century came chivalry, aristocratic, because only a man of noble blood could be a knight; protective, and not reforming. It fused the aristocratic and churchly forms of the protective spirit: for knighthood was personal, and could not be bequeathed, paralleling ecclesiastical celibacy. Out of this Europe owes those orders, half aristocratic, half religious, the Knights Templars, the Knights of St. James, the Knights of St. John, which inflicted the greatest evils on societies; and whose members, combining kindred vices, enlivened the superstitions of monks with the debaucheries of soldiers. Thus chivalry, uniting the principles of celibacy and noble birth, incarnated the spirit of the two classes to whom these principles belonged. The strength and duration of chivalry accordingly measure the strength of the protective spirit. Tournaments, first open expression of chivalry, are of French origin, and lasted until 1560. Personal vanity, an outgrowth of chivalry, has always badged the Frenchman rather than the Englishman; duelling, a custom springing from chivalry, was always more popular in France than England.

The class of nobles is always averse to innovations. Their eyes are turned to their pedigrees, their quarterings, their ancient ancestry, their ancestor who came over with the Norman or aided in the first invasion of Ireland: they associate grandeur with antiquity, and transfer to the past that admiration they should reserve for the future. What the nobles are to politics, the priests are to religion. They too rely on antiquity and tradition, and take for granted that what is old is better than what is new. When Elizabeth, on her accession, found that the ancient families held to the ancient religion, she naturally called to her councils advisers more likely to uphold the novelties that the age demanded. The two Bacons, the two Cecils, Knollys, Sadler, Smith, Throgmorton, Walsingham, were the most eminent statesmen and diplomats in her reign; and they were all commoners. The rebellion of 1569 was essentially an aristocratic movement: the bitterest enemy of Elizabeth was Mary of Scotland; and Mary's interests were publicly defended by the Duke of Norfolk, the Earls of Northumberland, Westmoreland, and Arundel, and secretly favored by the Marquis of Northampton, and the Earls of Pembroke, Derby, Cumberland, Shrewsbury, and Sussex. Cecil, Elizabeth's most powerful minister, studied the genealogies and resources of the great families, to increase his control over them; the Queen delighted in humbling them. Dignity of rank and purity of blood meant nothing to her: it was her degenerate successors who shrined such qualities. After her death, both James and Charles sought to revive the power of the nobles and the clergy: but the hour had passed, in England, when the protective spirit could control.

The Fronde and the English Rebellion.—The English Rebellion was a war of classes, as well as of factions. From the beginning, yeomen and traders adhered to the parliament; nobles and clergy rallied around the throne. The French rebellion shows no such large division. It too was a struggle of parliament against crown; an attempt to secure liberty, and chain despotism. The English parliamentary forces had a few nobles with them at first: the Earl of Essex was appointed general of the forces, the Earl of Bedford his lieutenant, while the Earl of Manchester was commissioned to raise troops. Essex fell out of favor, Bedford abandoned his forces, Manchester was legally deprived of power. The week after the execution of the king, the parliamentary party took away the legislative power of the peers, recording their opinion that the House of Lords is "useless, dangerous, and ought to be abolished."

The Rebellion was the work of men who looked before, and not behind. No dispute over ship-money or privileges of parliament caused it; the spirit of the people was responsible. Joyce, who abducted the king, had been a tailor; Colonel Pride, author of that legislative cathartic called "Pride's Purge," had been a drayman. The leaders of the "fifth monarchy men" were Venner, a wine-cooper; Tuffnel, a carpenter; and Okey, who rose from stoker in an Islington brewery to be a colonel. Cromwell himself was a brewer; Colonel Jones, his brother-in-law, a servant to a private gentleman. Deane was a tradesman's servant, and became an admiral, and commissioner of the navy; Colonel Goffe, apprentice to a drysalter; Skippon, an uneducated common soldier, was made commander of the London militia, sergeant-major-general of the army, and commander-in-chief of Ireland. Two lieutenants of the Tower were Berkstead, a pedlar, and Tichborne, a linen-draper. Colonel Harvey was a silk-mercer, as were Colonels Rowe and Venn; Salway, a grocer's apprentice. His fellow councillors included Bond the draper, Carley the brewer, Berners the private servant, Holland the link-boy. Among others promoted were Packe the woolen-draper, Pury the weaver, Pemble the tailor, Barebone the leather-seller. Downing, once a charity boy, became teller of the Exchecquer, and representative of England at the Hague. Colonel Horton had been a gentleman's servant; Colonel Berry, a wood-monger; Colonel Cooper, a haberdasher; Major Rolfe, a shoe-maker; Colonel Fox, a tinker; and Colonel Hewson, a cobbler.

Such were the instruments by which the English rebellion was consummated. In France, the rebels were headed by noble leaders. Instead of butchers, bakers, brewers, cobblers, and tinkers, we had aristocratic insurgents and titled dema-gogs like the Princes de Conde, de Conti, de Marsillac, the Dukes de Bouillon, de Beaufort, de Longueville, de Chevreuse, de Nemours, de Luynes, de Brissac, d'Elboeuf, de Candale, de la Trémouille, the Marquises de la Boulaye, de Laigues, de Noirmoutier, de Vitry, de Fosseuse, de Sillery, d'Estissac, d'Hocquincourt, and the Counts de Rantzau and de Mon-trésor. The English leaders were from the people, and pre-served the union of the whole party; in France, the sym-pathy was very weak, and the union very precarious. What sort of sympathy could there be between the mechanic and peasant, toiling for daily bread, and the rich and dissolute noble, whose life was passed in idle and frivolous pursuits which debased the mind, and made his order a by-word and reproach among the nations? These very nobles treated their inferiors with habitual and insolent contempt; unhappily for themselves, the people looked up to the nobles with the great-est veneration. The very fact that the people were incapable of conducting their own rebellion, and had to place them-selves under the command of the nobles, increased the servil-ity of the people; thus stunting the growth of freedom. The object of the people was to free themselves from the yoke; that of the nobles, to find new sources of excitement. The nobles did not have pride, the consciousness of self-applause; but vanity, which needs the applause of others. They had

vanity of the most despicable kind, their empty understand-
ings busied with ribands, stars, crosses, Garters; their ambition being to carry a wand at court, or to make daughter or
wife maid-of-honor or mistress of the queen's robes.

A few examples will indicate the quality of the French
nobles of the time. The right of sitting in the royal presence
was one of the vital claims. According to ancient French
court etiquette, a duke's wife might sit in the presence of
the queen, but even the wife of a marquis might not.
Marquises, counts, and other nobles strove for this privilege,
valiantly opposed by the dukes. Louis XIII made an un-
fortunte innovation, and allowed the privilege to female
members of the Bouillon family. The lower nobles pressed
the point; and in 1648 and 1649 the queen-regent granted
the right to the three most distinguished members of the
lower aristocracy, the Countess de Fleix, Madame de Pons,
and the Princess de Marsillac. Princes of the blood and peers
of the realm flocked to the capital, to rebuff this hideous innovation; the inferior nobles, flushed by this success, demanded that this right, given to the house of Foix, in the
person of the Countess de Fleix, should be granted to all of
equally illustrious pedigree. There was imminent danger that
the matter would be settled by armed insurrection. The
queen, however, sent word to the higher nobles, by four mar-
shals of France, that the privilege would be withdrawn: and
this had to be signed by her, and the four secretaries of state,
before the higher nobles would peaceably disperse.

French memoirs of the seventeenth century ring with such
immense problems as who should have an arm-chair at court,
who should be invited to the royal dinners, who was to be
kissed by the queen, who should have first seat in church, how
long should be the cloth on which various persons were to
stand; whether the Duke of Bouillon, who once possessed the
sovereignty of Sedan, was superior to the Duke de Roche-
foucauld, who never possessed any sovereignty at all; whether
the Duke de Beaufort ought to enter the council-chamber
before the Duke de Nemours, and whether, being there, he

ought to sit above him. Most absurd of all, serious misunderstandings arose as to who should have the honor of giving the king his napkin at meals, and who should possess the ineffable elevation of helping the queen on with her underthings. Such miserable matters form part of the history of the French mind; they rose from that bloating of the protective spirit which cursed France. The intellectual movement stimulated France to rebellion; this was neutralized by the habit of the people of looking up to the nobles, and of the nobles of looking up to the king.

Louis XIV: *The Protective Spirit in Literature.*—The protective spirit, as applied by Louis XIV to literature, meant that every man of letters became a vassal of the French crown; that every book was written with a view to the royal favor. This prince's reign, tried by the lowest standard of morals, of honor, or even of interest, must be utterly condemned. He formed a strict alliance with the church, leaving his people to be oppressed by the clergy. He revoked the Edict of Nantes; in order to frighten Protestants into conversion, he suddenly let loose upon them whole troops of dissolute soldiers, who were allowed to practice frightful cruelties. Protestants were bound on the rack, made drunk, and then converted to Catholicism; some were stripped stark naked, stuck with pins from head to foot, hacked with penknives, torn by the noses with red-hot pincers, and thus converted to Catholicism. Husbands and fathers were tied to bedposts, while the soldiers ravished their wives and daughters before their eyes, for the glory of the Father, the Son, the Holy Ghost, and the Virgin Mary. The nails of hands and feet were plucked from others; or the feet burnt off; or the bodies of men and women blown up with the bellows, till they were ready to burst. Half a million of the most industrious Frenchmen were forced to flee the land. Yet, in the face of such universally known facts, there are found men who hold up the reign of Louis XIV to admiration.

In his reign, every vestige of liberty was destroyed; the people were weighed down with insupportable taxation; the resources of the country were squandered riotously. The one defense for the realm is that, to counterbalance such evils, we have the Letters of Pascal, the Orations of Bossuet, the Comedies of Molière, the Tragedies of Racine. This error is connected with false notions concerning the influence of royal patronage upon national literature. Men of letters have been the first to propagate this delusion, holding that there is some magical power in the smile of a king, to quicken man's intellect. This is injurious to the independent spirit which literature should possess. Kings may be applauded in proportion as they add to the happiness of the nation they are called to rule over; but it should be remembered that their information must be inaccurate, and their prejudices numerous. They can not be judicious patrons of literature; we should be satisfied if they do not obstinately oppose the spirit of the times. Kings reward, not the most able, but the most compliant. A profound and independent thinker will be refused patronage granted to another, who cherishes ancient prejudices and defends ancient abuses. For one instance in which a king has rewarded a man in advance of his age, there are twenty in which he has recompensed one behind his age.

Hence, in every country where royal patronage has been long and generally bestowed, the spirit of literature, instead of being progressive, has become reactionary. The bounties artificially spawn a greedy and necessitous class, who, eager for pensions, offices, and titles, have made the pursuit of truth subordinate to the desire of gain, and have saturated their writings with the prejudices of the court before which they crouch. The mark of favor has become the badge of servitude. Moreover, excessive encouragement of writing may cause a supply in excess of the normal demand—a necessary result of protection in literature. If a royal fund rewarded butchers and tailors, the number of these useful men would be abnormally increased. The same is true of poets and novelists. An increase of authors is no more followed by a diffusion of knowledge, than an increase in butchers is followed by greater diffusion of food. What a government gives to one class, it must take from another. As literature is pensioned, wealth, and the lower classes, are depressed: all is splendid above, all rotten below. Even the pensioned class soon decays; men who begin by losing their independence, soon lose their energy. That intellect is robust indeed, which does not wither in the sickly atmosphere of a court. The attention of authors being concentrated on their master, they insensibly contract the servility suitable to their position: which becomes a custom and a pleasure to their diseased and warped natures. Literature soon loses its boldness, the spirit of inquiry is extinguished. Then the minds of men, finding no outlet, rankle into a deadly hatred: until they burst into blood and destruction, whose long arm stabs to the heart of the palace.

The people must take heed, that literary men's interests are on their side, instead of on the side of the rulers. Literature represents the intellect, which is progressive; government represents order, which is stationary. If these powers coalesce, if government corrupts the intellect, and intellect cringes before government, the result must be despotism in politics, and servility in literature. This was the history of France under Louis XIV. The king's reputation originated in the gratitude of men of letters; it is fostered by the idea that the celebrated literature of the age is due to his care. Two circumstances indicate that this literature was the result of the king's predecessors. The first is that, after Louis XIV's grasp of power in 1661, until his death in 1715, no great discovery was made in France. Descartes, Pascal, Fermat, Gassendi, Mersenne, functioned during the seventeenth century; but these men investigated while the king was in his cradle, and finished before he assumed the government. After the king assumed his power, French scientific research stopped. Louis heard that astronomy was a noble study, and invited to his court the greatest foreign astronomers: so dead was France, that Newton's great discoveries were not adopted by any French astronomer until forty-five years after they were published, or 1732. There was a similar absence of practical ingenuity in France. Pecquet's great discovery of the receptacle of the chyle was made in 1647, when the king was nine years old; the great anatomist Riolan published his last work before the king was fifteen. In surgery, zoology, chemistry, botany, the record is similarly blank.

The age of Louis was an age of decay, misery, intolerance, oppression, bondage, utter incompetence. As the national intellect declined, the misery and degradation of country and people followed. Royalty and nobles, intensely busied with their picayune affairs, have no time to understand the working of intellect; and in the bestowal of awards they are bound to go wrong. Science was sacrificed to art; and art itself soon decayed. The few achievers were born and educated under his freer predecessors. Everything of value was done in the first half of his reign; the second half, which should have showed the flowering of his policy, showed universal sterility in art. The painters, architects, sculptors, poets, died and left no successors. Racine, Molière, Boileau, Pascal, Corneille, all dated in the beginning, not the noon, of the reign of Louis. As a result of the protective spirit in literature, men of letters degenerated into a fawning and hypocritical race, who opposed all improvement, and supported every old abuse. There was no popular liberty; there were no great men; no science, no literature, no arts. Within, there was a discontented people, a greedy government, a bankrupt treasury; without, there were foreign armies crowding upon the frontiers, which were barely prevented from dismembering France. By seeking to concentrate on his single person the glory of France, his policy gained the admiration of intellect, made it courtly and sycophantic, and ended by destroying all their boldness, stifling original thought, and postponing for an indefinite period the progress of national civilization.

Preparations for the French Revolution.—At last Louis XIV died. The people went almost mad with joy. There followed a reaction unparalleled in modern history. The forced hypocrisy gave way to the grossest licentiousness. A few high-spirited youths saw beyond the gambling house and the brothel, and turned their eyes toward "the only country where freedom was practiced," England: a movement giving rise to that junction of English and French intellects which is, from its results, the most important fact in the history of the eighteenth century. During the time between the death of Louis XIV and the Revolution, there was hardly a Frenchman of eminence who did not visit England. Buffon, Brissot, Gournay, Helvétius, Lalande, Lafayette, Montesquieu, Morellet, Mirabeau, Madame Roland, Rousseau, Ségur, Voltaire—these, and scores of lesser ability, visited England, studied the language, seized the spirit of the literature. Voltaire greedily imbibed, popularized in France the philosophy of Newton, recommended Locke, Shakespeare, and had read extensively. More than a hundred prominent French writers can be named who were at this time familiar with the English language and its authors, as their references attest.

Those who took part in actually consummating the Revolution were moved by the prevailing spirit. Lafayette, Camille Desmoulins, Marat, Mirabeau, Le Brun, Brissot, Condorcet, Madame Roland, the Duke of Orleans, were inspired by English liberty: it was in the society of London that Orleans acquired the taste for liberty, for popular agitation, as well as contempt for his own rank, and familiarity with those beneath. It was English literature which taught political liberty, first to France, and through France to the rest of Europe. These eminent Frenchmen found peculiarities in England unheard of at home. Bold debates upon political and religious questions amazed them, and inspired them to carry into their own writings something of the English spirit.

The French nobles and clergy, so long accustomed to power, commenced a crusade against knowledge which forms the second principal precursor of the French Revolution. This was a prolonged and systematic attempt to stifle all inquiry, and punish all inquirers. Of all the literary men who wrote in the ninety years after the death of Louis XIV, nine out of every ten suffered from the government some grave injury. Among those who suffered confiscation, or imprisonment, or

exile, or fines, or the suppression of their works, or the igno-
miny of being forced to recant, were Beaumarchais, Buffon,
D'Alembert, Diderot, Helvétius, Mably, Marmontel, Montesquieu, Rousseau, Suard, and Voltaire. Voltaire was jailed,
grossly insulted by a duke, beaten on the streets, jailed again,
and exiled. Books were banned for the most puerile reasons.
Rousseau was threatened with prison, was exiled, had his books
publicly burnt. Buffon had to recant his geological views
to satisfy the clergy. Thousands of books were ordered to be
burned by the public hangman. Diderot was jailed for writing that men born blind had different ideas from men born
with eyes. One more instance should be cited to show how
the authorities interfered with even domestic affairs. An
actress named Chantilly married Favart, a song-writer, although Maurice de Saxe desired to make her his mistress.
Maurice applied for aid to the French crown: the government
of France ordered Favart to abandon his wife, and to intrust
her to the adulterous embrace of Maurice, to which she had
to submit.

The delay of the Revolution, in the face of these mountain-
ous oppressions, is one of the striking facts of history; and
indicates how the habit of slavery clings to man like a fetter-
ing chain. In 1764, the government forbade the publication of any book discussing questions of government; in 1767,
it was made a capital offense to write a book likely to excite
the public mind; the same penalty applied to one who attacked religion, or spoke of matters of finance. It was proposed by a crown officer to do away with all publishers, and
allow books only to be published by the king's press. Yet
literature was the only resource of liberty in France. There
was no free press, free parliament, free debates, public meetings, popular suffrage, habeas corpus act, trial by jury.

French revolutionary literature was first directed against
religion, rather than against politics. For forty years the
church was attacked, and the crown spared. This was because of the lowered position of the French clergy, and the
high esteem of the kings. Only one English king, Alfred,

sometimes called the Great, has a title of popular admiration; France had Louis the Mild, Louis the Saint, Louis the Just, Louis the Great, and the most vicious of all was called Louis the Beloved. The political oppression of the French crown was protected by the rooted strength of popular prejudices; the boldest thinker at first never thought of attacking it. The clergy, after Louis XIV, were dissolute and ignorant, and this was another reason why they were attacked. Opposition to religion naturally tended to lower it in the minds of the opponents; they attacked not the vices of the clergy alone, but religion and Christianity itself. If the rulers had listened, the church might have fallen, but the state itself might have been saved. By the middle of Louis's reign, France became so democratic that the revolution became inevitable.

In vain the crown called in men like Turgot and Necker, whose wise and liberal proposals would, a little earlier, have calmed the popular agitation. It was in vain that the Jesuits were suppressed, promises made to reform the grievances, and even the states general summoned, for the first time in a hundred and seventy years. The time for treaty had gone by: the time for battle had come.

CHAPTER VII

HISTORICAL LITERATURE AND THE FRENCH REVOLUTION

History in France, 1599-1799.—In historical writing, the first condition of progress is doubt. Man's doubt appears first in religion; then, when theology decays, literary heresies become more common. Until 1599, France had not produced a single historian because she had not produced a single man who presumed to doubt what was generally believed. The first critical digest was Du Haillan's history of the kings of France, appearing in 1576. His sourcebook was a gossipy Italian compilation of historical fables; and Du Haillan adds his own inventions to his sources. The first history composed by a Frenchman was De Thou's, appearing in 1604; Sully was his contemporary, and both were moved by the spirit of scepticism. Serres, in 1597, first insisted upon recording the date of each event; Scipio Dupleix, in 1621, published the evidence for each fact with the fact itself. In 1599, La Popelinière critically examined the works of other historians; and formally refuted the fable, so dear to early historians, by which France was founded by Francus, who arrived in Gaul after the siege of Troy.

More than such minor histories was Mézeray's History of France, appearing 1643-1651. His especial merits are an indisposition to believe strange things, merely because they had hitherto been believed; and an inclination to take the side of the people, rather than the rulers. His example was not followed in the second particular, since Louis XIV came to the throne, and a dearth of historians was one result of his protective patronage of literature. When Louis came to the throne Mézeray was still living, and received a crown pension of four thousand francs. In 1668 he published an abridgement of his history, with remarks on the tendency of taxation which caused offense in high quarters. When it was found he was too honest and fearless to retract, half his pension was taken from him, and then the other half. In 1681 the Abbé Primi, an Italian, was induced to write a history of Louis XIV. The king liberally rewarded the man in advance; but the completed book was found to contain several indiscreet disclosures. For this, the book was suppressed, and the historian thrown into the Bastille. The king ordered Racine and Boileau to write accounts of his reign, promising to supply them with the necessary materials. The shrewd writers took the pensions, but omitted to write the history. In 1683, the Englishman Burnet was made a similar offer, to write a history "on the side of the king."

From these facts it is easy to see why historical writing declined. It may have become more elegant; it became unquestionably more feeble. Every king was made a hero, every bishop a saint. Unpleasant truth was suppressed: but with this, independence, boldness, life were gone. A typical history was Audigier's celebrated work on the Origin of the French, published at Paris in 1676. This great work told how, 3,464 years after the creation of the world, and 590 years before the birth of Christ, Sigovese, nephew to the king of the Celts, was first sent into Germany. These were the Vandals, from the German "wandeln," to go. Jupiter, Pluto, and Neptune, whom some suppose to be gods, were really kings of Gaul. Gallus, founder of Gaul, was no other than Noah himself. Alexander the Great never dared attack the Scythians, a colony sent from France. The English are merely a French colony, as the similarity of Angles and Anjou proves. French kings for fifteen centuries were really emperors, and at the same time superior to emperors. Antichrist will never appear in the world until the French empire is destroyed; as many saints testified, and St. Paul himself indicated, in Second Thessalonians.

The enlightened age of Louis XIV swallowed all this. Bossuet made history merely a handmaid of theology; he takes everything for granted which the church had been accustomed to believe. His slavish acceptance of Vulgate chronologies is only excelled by the learned Dr. Stukeley, who wrote in 1730: "According to my calculations, I find God Almighty ordered Noah to get the creatures into the ark on Sunday, the twelfth of October, the very day of the autumnal equinox that year; and on this present day, on the Sunday se'nnight following (the nineteenth of October) that terrible catastrophe began, the moon being past her third quarter." In ancient history, he devoted his emphasis to the Jews; he omits Mohammedanism entirely. He delighted to taunt the human intellect; he eulogized, not men of intellect, but conquerors, those pests and destroyers of men.

After Louis's death the change is impressive. Voltaire's first study, a life of Charles XII, was written in the servile tradition of the preceding generation: yet at least he had emerged from the supernatural shadow in which Bossuet moved. His next work was called the *Age of Louis XIV*: not the peculiarities of a prince, but the movements of a people. He has one chapter on commerce and internal government; another on finances; another on the history of science; and three on the progress of the fine arts. Four years later appeared his *Morals, Manners, and Character of Nations*. "I wish," said Voltaire, "to write a history, not of wars, but of society; and to ascertain how men lived within their families, and what were the arts which they commonly cultivated." For, he adds, "my object is the history of the human mind. . . . I want to know what were the steps by which men passed from barbarism to civilization." The same tendency is found in Montesquieu and Turgot, contemporaries of Voltaire; in Mallet, whose history of Denmark appeared in 1755; in Balby, whose History of France appeared in 1765. Velly, Villaret, Duclos, even the courtly Henault, belonged to the same school of historical writing.

Voltaire was the first historian who endeavored, by large

views, to explain the origin of feudalism; he was the author of the profound remark that licentious religious ceremonies have no connection with licentious national morals. He recommended universal free trade; he punctured the adulation lavished on the Middle Ages, which he represented as they were: a period of ignorance, ferocity, and licentiousness, when injuries were unredressed, crime unpunished, and superstition unrebuked. He turned his attack upon the false dignity given to classical scholars over writers upon contemporary themes—an attack packed with wit and ridicule. "Voltaire did more than any other man to sap the foundation of ecclesiastical power, and to destroy the supremacy of classical studies." The absurd earthly mythic history of Rome, then accepted as true, was demolished by Voltaire. Taking him on the whole, "he is probably the greatest historian Europe has yet produced."

Montesquieu exhibits the same spirit, especially in the rejection of personal anecdotes, and his union of the history of man and the physical sciences. He knew that, in the great march of human affairs, human peculiarities count for nothing; he knew that such physical considerations as climate, soil, and food deeply affected man's history. His conclusions in this field failed, because the state of physical sciences was backward; his great contribution lay in the method. Turgot's celebrated lectures, in which he was said to have created the philosophy of history, came at the same time. His method is identical with Montesquieu's; and though thereafter his participation in public life kept him from filling in the splendid outline he had sketched out, yet he should be mentioned as one of the chief expressions of the new spirit in historical writing.

Religion and Atheism.—The great Frenchmen of the eighteenth century had refrained from attacking the government, and had levelled all their fire against the church, for causes already indicated. It is hard to fix the exact date when their attack altered and was focussed on the state; the dates of great intellectual revolutions cannot be ascertained as easily as the birth of a king, or the death of a pope. Yet 1750 may be fixed as the time when the agitations that caused the French Revolution entered upon their second stage, the political stage. In 1750 the French commenced their great studies on political economy; books on finance and other problems of government multiplied. Within twenty years, even fashionable conversation no longer turned upon new poems and plays, but upon political questions. When Necker, in 1781, published his celebrated Report on the Finances of France, 6,000 copies were sold the first day, and two presses were kept constantly running to supply the demand. Rousseau began publishing after the middle of the century; and he abstained from attacks on Christianity, exerting himself only against the civil and political abuses of the times. Before 1750, not a single great French writer attacked political problems; after that date such attacks were frequent. After 1750 the only French writers who still assailed the clergy, and refused to interfere in politics, were those who, like Voltaire, had reached an advanced age, and had drawn their ideas from the preceding generation. Most significant of all, is that the same year marked a change in the policy of the government. The crown turned decisively against the church, at the very time that the writers turned against the crown.

The attacks of the writers had weakened the church; it was natural that the government should step in and plunder it, in its enfeebled condition. In 1749 the first step against the church was taken; and Machault, the new controller-general and chancellor, turned next to tax the property of the clergy. His successors continued the policy; and the government as a whole began to favor that great doctrine of religious liberty. The church itself was divided by a great internal squabble, one faction of which sided with the state against the other churchly party. In 1787 a churchman, Brienne, archbishop of Toulouse, who was then minister, laid before parliament a royal edict, removing all disabilities against Protestants. Moreover, soon after the middle of the century, the crown inflicted a direct and fatal injury upon the spiritual authority, in the expulsion of the Jesuits. For the first fifty years after its installation, this society had benefited society, especially by installing a system of education far superior to any yet seen in Europe. By the eighteenth century, they had begun to check that knowledge which, two centuries before, they had labored to spread.

No point has provoked hotter disputes among metaphysicians than the respective merits of free will and good works. From the time of Athanasius, Christianity has had two rival camps, one denying the freedom of the will; the other upholding it, and insisting upon good works as essential to salvation. The first theory was upheld by Calvin and others; the second, by Arminius and his followers. The first spirit, called Calvinism in England, has always been connected with the democratic spirit; the doctrine of Arminism has been most favored by the aristocratic or protective party. The ecclesiastical party espoused Arminianism, the Puritans and Independents were Calvinistic. Calvinism is essentially a doctrine for the poor; Arminianism, for the rich. In Calvinism, belief is enough for salvation; and the poorest man can afford this. Under Arminianism, salvation is sought by rich gifts; only the rich can shine in this. This affects the church practice: every Christian democracy has simplified worship, every Christian aristocracy has embellished it. Moreover, Calvinism is more favorable to the sciences, and thinkers; and Arminianism, to the arts, and to scholars. Calvinists, fixing their attention on their own minds, are narrower, but less servile.

The revival of Jansenism in France in the eighteenth century is significant; for Jansenism was a form of Calvinism. There appeared that inquisitive, democratic, and insubordinate spirit, which has always accompanied the creed. The great opponents of the Jesuits, Machault, Turgot, Necker, Rousseau, and the rest, were Jansenists, or leaned in that direction. It became impossible that the Jesuits should hold their ground. The last defenders of authority and tradition, they must fall in an age when the statesmen were sceptics, and the theologians Calvinists. Even the people marked them for destruction: when Damiens, in 1757, attempted to assassinate the king, it was erroneously believed that they had instigated the act. In April, 1761, parliament ordered their constitutions to be laid before it. In August they were forbidden to receive novices, their colleges were closed, and many of their most celebrated works were burned by the public hangman. In 1762 they were condemned without being heard in their own defense; their property was directed to be sold, and their order disbanded and formally abolished. The alleged cause was their ill-faith in a commercial transaction, the fraudulent repudiation of a common debt. They were not charged with plotting against the state, or corrupting public morals, or overturning religion: these were unnecessary in the eighteenth century. Yet the cause was not the bankruptcy of a trader, or the intrigues of a mistress: their real crime was that they belonged to the past, rather than the present.

After the fall of the Jesuits, it seemed plain that the French church must fall next. Men of ability had ceased to labor in it. They had no active leaders; they had lost the confidence of government, the respect of the people. Yet for thirty years they were able to maintain their standing, and to interfere unpunished in affairs of government. One reason was that leading Frenchmen were beginning to attack the crown, and had slackened their onslaughts against the church. Thus at no period did the speculative thinkers and the practical classes unite against the church in France. Men had become atheists, and so no longer troubled about mere perversions of religion. In 1751 appeared the celebrated Encyclopedia, openly promulgating atheism. The opinions spread rapidly. In 1770 appeared the *System of Nature,* which has justly been called the code of atheism. In 1775 the Archbishop of Toulouse, formally addressing the king, stated that atheism had now become the prevailing opinion. Atheism was openly advocated by Condorcet, D'Alembert, Diderot, Helvétius, Lalande, Laplace, Mirabeau, and Saint Lambert. In 1764 Hume met, at the house of Baron d'Holbach, a party of the most celebrated Frenchmen residing in Paris. The great

Scotchman raised the subject of atheism, and said he had never chanced to meet an atheist. "You have been somewhat unfortunate," said Holbach, "but at the present moment you are sitting at table with seventeen of them."

"This, sad as it is, only forms a single aspect of that immense movement, by which" the French mind, during the latter half of the eighteenth century, was drawn from the study of the internal world, to be concentrated upon the external. In 1758 appeared that essay on "the Mind," which bears the same relation to ethics that atheism bears to theology. Helvétius in this credits our difference from animals solely upon our bodily structure. All notions of duty and virtue must be tested by their relations to the senses; in other words, by the gross amount of physical enjoyment to which they give rise. Our vices and our virtues are solely the result of our passions; and our passions are caused by our physical sensibility to pain and to pleasure. The loftiest virtues, as well as the meanest vices, are equally caused by the pleasure we find in the use of them. Such views furnish a clue to the movements of this remarkable age. Madame Dudeffand expressed the effect on the popular mind, when she said that Helvétius was popular, since he told to men all their own secrets. In 1754, Condillac produced his celebrated work on the mind, the *Treatise on Sensations;* in which he stated that everything we know is the result of sensation—is an effect produced on us by the action of the external world. The faculties of men, he says, are solely caused by the operation of man's senses. In man, nature is the beginning of all; to nature we owe the whole of our knowledge.

The Physical Sciences.—In France, during the latter half of the eighteenth century, the idea was, the inferiority of the internal to the external. This dangerous but plausible principle drew the attention of men from the church to the state; it also drew men to a study of nature's laws, and caused the discovery of "more new truths concerning the external world. . . . than during all the previous periods put together," at least in France. The three most important forces by which the operations of nature are effected are heat, light, and electricity. In all three fields the French exerted themselves with signal success. The laws of radiation of heat were worked out by Prévost; of its conduction, by Fourier. In electricity, the experiment of D'Alibard and Coulomb brought electrical phenomena under the jurisdiction of mathematics. As to light, Malus discovered its polarization, the most splendid contribution received by optical science since the analysis of the sun's rays. Moreover, Fresnel began the researches which placed on a solid basis the great wave theory, which overthrew the Newtonian theory of the corpuscular nature of light.

The immense value of these discoveries is incontestable; yet discoveries were made in fields more easily understood, which showed a remarkable influence in strengthening that democratic tendency which accompanied the French Revolution. The fields of chemistry and geology refer to the composition of matter and its position. The first deals with the properties of matter; the second, with its location. Chemistry deals with the molecular arrangement of the smallest atoms; geology with the arrangements in the universe of the largest masses. If we knew all the laws in both fields, we should know all the changes of which matter is spontaneously capable, that is, when uninterrupted by the mind of man.

We owe to France the existence of chemistry as a science, that is, as a body of generalizations so true, that these may be absorbed later into higher generalizations, but may never be overthrown. The history of chemistry has shown only three stages: (1) the destruction of the phlogistic theory, and the establishment upon its ruins of the doctrines of oxidation, combustion, and respiration; (2) the establishment of the principle of definite proportions, and the application to it of the atomic hypothesis; and (3) the union of chemical and electrical laws, and progress toward fusing into one generalization both sets of phenomena. The first of these stages was the work of Lavoisier, greatest of French chemists. He not only worked out the laws of the oxidation of bodies and their combustion, but was the author of the true theory of respiration, as a purely chemical process.

In geology, Buffon's theory, dating from the middle of the eighteenth century, was followed by the researches of many French minds, which familiarized the French people with the strange conception, that the surface of our planet, even where it appears perfectly stable, is constantly undergoing the most extensive changes. At this point the subject was taken up by Cuvier, one of the greatest naturalists Europe has ever produced. He founded geology as a science. He was the first to bring upon it the generalizations of comparative anatomy, the study of the framework of animals; he was the first to coordinate the study of the strata of the earth with the study of the fossil animals found in them. Before his time, the primary strata had been investigated by the Germans, the secondary ones by the English. But these investigations were isolated. From the French we received our knowledge of the tertiary strata, in which the remains of organic life are most numerous, and in which the general likeness to the present or quarternary stage is closest. The first application of comparative anatomy to the study of fossil skeletons was the work of a Frenchman, the celebrated Daubenton. Before his time, the bones had merely excited wonder: some saying they were rained from heaven, others, that they were the gigantic limbs of the ancient patriarchs, who were believed to be tall because the old historians had said that they were superhumanly old. Daubenton's Memoir, published in 1762, forever destroyed such idle conceits—another evidence of the state of the French mind.

By this union of geology and anatomy, there was first introduced into the study of nature a clear view of the magnificent doctrine of universal change, as well as a conception of the regularity of the changes, and of the unchanging laws by which they are governed. We now see that the same regularity must have existed long before our little planet assumed its present form, and long before man walked the face of the earth. Thus in astronomy we are able to predict events before they actually happen: the burden of proof lies now, not on those who assert the eternal regularity of nature, but on those who deny it. England diffused a love of freedom; France a knowledge of physical science; .and Germany and Scotland revived metaphysics, and created the study of philosophic history.

In zoology we owe to Frenchmen of the eighteenth century the highest generalizations this branch of knowledge has reached. Zoology has two divisions: anatomy, the static or stationary part, and physiology, the dynamic or active part; the studies of the structure of animals, and of their functions. Both of these were worked out, at nearly the same time, by Cuvier and Bichat. In 1795 Cuvier laid down the great principle, that animals must be classified, not by external peculiarities, but by internal organization. Thus he overthrew the artificial system of Linnaeus. Great as was his achievement, that of Bichat was greater. He must be pronounced the most profound thinker and the most consummate observer by whom the organization of the animal frame has yet been studied. He saw that it was necessary to study, not merely the organs, but the tissues of which these organs were constructed; his researches "are probably the most valuable contribution ever made to physiology by a single mind." In 1801 he published his great study of the tissues. The body of man, he points out, possesses twenty-one different tissues, alike in their properties of extensibility and contractility. He examined these tissues under every sort of experimental condition. Agassiz, following Bichat, found that fossil fishes could only be classified by tissue analysis, since the organs had been destroyed: and found that, if all of a fish but one membrane had been destroyed, it was practicable from this membrane to reconstruct the animal in its most essential parts. A similar discovery was that the teeth of an animal have a necessary connection with the entire organization of its frame; so that, within certain limits, we can predict the organization by examining one tooth.

After all, our highest admiration must go, not to those

who make the discoveries themselves, but rather to those who·point out how the discoveries are to be made. Every department of knowledge in application reveals itself in inventions, discoveries, and method, which correspond to art, to science, and to philosophy. The highest of these is the philosophy of method. Thus Bichat's work, like all men of the highest eminence—Aristotle, Bacon, and Descartes—marks an epoch in the history of the human mind. In geology, the followers of Bichat are associated with the doctrine of uniformity; in zoology, with that of transmutation of species; in astronomy, with the nebular hypothesis.

Bichat's most valuable production aimed at nothing less than an exhaustive generalization of the functions of life. Life as a whole consists of two branches: animal and vegetable. That confined to animals alone is called animal; that common to both is called organic life. In the organic life, man exists solely for himself: in the animal life, he comes in contact with others. The functions of the first are purely internal, those of the second, external. Organic life is limited to creation and destruction: the first consisting of assimilation, as digestion, circulation, and nutrition; the second of excretion, such as exhalation and the like. Man has this in common with plants; of this life he, in a natural state, is unconscious. But the characteristic of his animal life is consciousness, by which he is made capable of moving, of feeling, of judging. The first life makes him a vegetable; the second, an animal.

We next note that the organs of his vegetable life are very irregular, while those of his animal life are symmetrical. His vegetative or organic life is conducted by the stomach, the intestines, and the glandular system, such as liver and pancreas; all of which are irregular. The animal organs are essentially symmetrical: the brain, the organs of sense, eyes,' nose, ears, are symmetrical; they as well as other organs of animal life, like feet and hands, are double. Thus animal functions may take rest; but, in organic life to stop is to die. The vegetable part of our body admits of no interruption, the animal is essentially intermittent. Thus the latter is capable of improvement, which the former is not. The first cry of the infant evolves into the perfect speech of man; but vegetable functions, existing in man several months before he is born, while they may increase in size, never really improve in function. The progressiveness of animal life is due to its intermittence; the unprogressiveness of organic life, to its continuity. This great work Bichat achieved, and since his time the field has remained practically stationary.

In botany we have only two generalizations wide enough to be called laws of nature: the beautiful law of form, that the different organs arise from arrested development, stamens, pistils, corolla, calyx, being merely stages of the leaf—a discovery made in Germany by Goethe; and the general knowledge of their structure, which we owe to eighteenth century Frenchmen. In crystallography, a branch of mineralogy, Romé de Lisle and Hauy, two eighteenth century Frenchmen, made invaluable discoveries, laying the foundations for a discovery of the pathology, or study of diseased states, in the inorganic world. Pinel's study of insanity is another great product of the time.

Thus the French Revolution was preceded by a complete change in the habits and associations of the national intellect. A vast social movement went on at the same time. Before the Revolution, the upper classes looked down with scorn upon the lower classes. The only three real sources of superiority—of morals, of intellect, and of knowledge—were entirely overlooked in the entire scheme. The cultivation of physical science began to reach the more unthinking parts of society. Discoveries in science began to be discussed by laborers as well as women of fashion. When the social orders met to discuss the same object, they became knit together by a new sympathy. "The highest and most durable of all pleasures, that caused by the perception of fresh truths," linked social elements formerly isolated.

A sign of this was the alteration in dress. In the seventeenth century, a man's rank might be known at once by his appearance: no one presumed to adopt a garb worn by the class above his own. In Paris, the dress became so simple as to cause a confusion of rank; until the men wore common frock coats, the women their ordinary morning gowns, even to formal social gatherings. The institution of clubs was another sign of the time. All the members of such clubs were, to some degree, educated; thus the distinction between noble and ignoble was succeeded by another division between educated and uneducated.

The first clubs were formed in 1782, seven years before the Revolution. The sexes were separated in these clubs; women associated more with each other, and were often seen in public unaccompanied by men; which encouraged among men a republican roughness, which the presence of women would have kept down. About 1784, the clubs became political. In 1787 orders were issued to close the leading club; but it was found impossible to stem the torrent. And then, in 1776, had occurred the American Declaration of Independence, which held the object of government was to secure the rights of the people, that the people gave it its powers; and that revolution was justified when government became destructive of these ends. A generation before, France would have rejected this with scorn; now, she welcomed it. When Franklin arrived in 1776 the government signed an alliance with him; and this contact with their new allies further stimulated the French democratic movement. Lafayette borrowed from America that famous doctrine respecting the rights of man, which, at his instigation, was formally adopted by the National Assembly. It is said that the advice of Jefferson caused the popular part of the legislative body to proclaim itself as the National Assembly, and thus set the crown at open defiance. This closes the survey of the causes of the French Revolution.

CHAPTER VIII

Loyalty and Superstition in Spain.—So far, four leading ing propositions have been established, which are to be regarded as the basis of the history of civilization. They are: (1) The progress of mankind depends on the success with which the laws of phenomena are investigated, and on the extent to which a knowledge of these laws is diffused. (2) Before such investigation can begin, a spirit of doubt or scepticism must arise, which aids the investigation, and is afterwards aided by it. (3) Discoveries thus made increase the influence of intellectual truths, and diminish relatively the influence of moral truths; moral truths being more stationary than intellectual truths, and receiving fewer additions. (4) The great enemy of this movement, and of civilization, is the protective spirit, or the idea that the state must teach men what to do, and the church, what they are to believe.

We have seen that the old tropical civilizations were accompanied by exaggerated Aspects of Nature, which inflamed the imagination, encouraged civilization, and prevented the creation of the physical sciences. No European country is so similar to the tropics as Spain. Nature has designed the land as the seat and refuge of superstition. The chief characteristics of the climate are heat and dryness. The rivers are in beds too deep to water the soil, which has remained arid. Droughts and famines are more serious than elsewhere in Europe. Sudden changes in the climate make it unhealthy; and in the middle ages, famine and pestilence were frequent; while earthquakes have been numerous. The climate renders it impossible for the agricultural laborer to work the whole of the day; this has caused an irregularity and instability of purpose, which made the people turn to the wandering avocation of a shepherd, rather than the more fixed pursuit of agriculture. The long Mahometan domination was accompanied by such frequent attacks, that agriculture was unwise, and pastoral pursuits inevitable.

Other and more influential events, tending in the same direction, became interwoven with these, and made the degradation of the country inevitable. After the overturn of the Roman Empire, Spain was settled by the Arian Visigoths, heretics in the eyes of Athanasian Roman Catholicism. For a hundred and fifty years this heresy flourished, attacked by the neighboring Franks, who were orthodox, and who were encouraged by their clergy to assail the dissenters. Under Clovis and his successors, the Frankish attacks threatened the existence of the Visigothic empire. Thus a war for national independence became also a war for national religion, and caused an intimate alliance between Arian kings and Arian clergy. The clergy gained by this, being well repaid for prayers against the enemy, and for their occasional miracles. This laid the foundation for the immense power of the Spanish priesthood.

Late in the sixth century, the Latin clergy converted their Visigothic masters; and the Spanish goverment, becoming orthodox, granted to its clerical teachers the power the Arian clergy had had, and, out of gratitude, even more power. Before the middle of the seventh century, the clergy here had more influence than anywhere in Europe. At a council in Toledo in 633, the king prostrated himself on the ground before the bishops; this became an established custom. The same process spread. Any layman, plaintiff or defendant, could insist on his case being tried by the bishop, instead of the secular judges. If both parties preferred the judges, the bishop could step in and reverse the judgment, if he regarded it as incorrect. Laws against heretics were harsher here than anywhere in Europe; the Jews being especially persecuted with unrelenting rigor. The king himself owed his throne to the bishops, who would acknowledge no king who did not promise to uphold their power.

In 711 the Mohammedans sailed from Africa, landed in south Spain, and in three years conquered all the land, except the almost inaccessible northwest. The Spaniards soon rallied here, and began to assail the invaders. A desperate struggle followed, which lasted 800 years. Again in Spain a war for national independence became a war for religion. Slowly the Christians fought their way. By the middle of the ninth century they reached the line of the Douro. Before the close of the eleventh they conquered as far as the Tagus; Toledo, their ancient capital, fell into their hands in 1085. Not until the capture of Malaga in 1487, and Granada in 1492, was the Christian empire reestablished, and the old Spanish monarchy restored. Thus Spain had had eight centuries of religious crusade. In camp and council-chamber the clergy were heard and obeyed. In the mountain retreat was preserved a chest filled with relics of the saints, the possession of which they regarded as their greatest security. By its aid the Spaniards believed that they gained miraculous victories. Looking upon themselves as soldiers of the cross, they became used to supernatural interference in everything.

Thus the course of events extended the power of the clergy. In the mountains of Asturias, the Spaniards soon lost what little civilization they had once had. They relapsed into barbarism; as their ignorance increased, so did their superstition. The Moslem invasion made the Christians poor; poverty caused ignorance, ignorance caused credulity, or a spirit of belief; this encouraged a reverential habit, and confirmed that habit of submission, that blind obedience to the church, which is the most unfortunate and important peculiarity of Spanish history. The theological element became the national character itself. The war with Granada, late in the fifteenth century, was theological far more than political; the purpose of Isabella and Ferdinand was not so much the acquisition of territory, as the propagation of the Christian faith. Scarcely was the war over, when the sovereigns issued a decree expelling from the country every Jew who refused to deny his faith, so that the soil of Spain might be polluted by no more unbelievers. To make them Christians, or, failing that, to exterminate them, was the business of the Inquisition, established in the same reign, and in full blast before the end of the 15th century.

During the 16th century, the throne was occupied by two princes of eminent ability, who pursued the same course. Charles V, who succeeded Ferdinand in 1516, governed Spain for forty years. His three principal wars were against France, the German princes, and Turkey; the latter two of these were religious. At the battle of Muhlberg, his humbling of the Protestant German princes retarded for some time the progress of the Reformation. His repulse of the Turks before Vienna was, in the east, what the expulsion of the Moors from Granada was to the west. From 50,000 to 100,000 persons were put to death in the Netherlands, during his reign, by his forces, on account of their religious opinions. His laws, 1520-1550, proclaimed that those convicted of heresy should be beheaded, or burned alive, or buried alive. This barbarous policy came, not from his vices of temperament, but from the large general causes already indicated.

Philip II, who succeeded Charles V in 1555, was the most perfect type of the national character. His favorite maxim, which is the key to his character, was, "It is better not to reign at all than to reign over heretics." He made every effort to stifle the Protestant heresy when it appeared in Spain, and killed it completely. The Dutch wished to adopt the reformed doctrine; Philip waged cruel war against them for thirty years, until his death. He ordered that every heretic who refused to recant should be burned. Even if he recanted, he must still die. His general, Alva, boasted that, in the five or six years of his administration, he had put to death in cold blood more than eighteen thousand men in the Low Countries, besides a larger number slain on the field of battle. We know that in one year more than 8,000 were executed or burned; Alva's total of 40,000 is probably not far from the truth. He fitted out at incredible cost the famous Armada, to humble England and nip European heresy in its bud, by depriving Protestants of their chief support and safe refuge.

The people acquiesced in this monstrous system, and cordially favored it. The arrogant king required even the most powerful nobles to address him only while on their knees; he spoke only in half sentences, leaving them to guess the rest. Yet the Spanish loved, reverenced, and adored such a monarch. Thus this harsh master, brutal parent, and bloody and remorseless ruler, became the object of adoring loyalty,—the quality which badges the Spaniard above any other European. A leading cause of this was the immense power of the clergy; for loyalty grows with superstition, and decays with it. This only fails when a despot breaks with the clergy, setting loyalty against superstition, as in Scotland. The Spanish spirit of loyalty was augmented by the great Arab invasion. The old ballads reflect this, being full of the national history. Such a poem was *The Cid*, written at the end of the 12th century. The drama could not represent an act of rebellion on the stage. No one might mount a horse, or marry a mistress, who had once belonged to the king. After his death, a king's widow could not marry. The spirit lasted in Spain until after the 18th century. This country, plagued with loyalty and superstition, was by nature isolated from the rest of Europe. At first, these forces produced a result apparently beneficial and certainly magnificent. From the broken condition of 1478, to 1590, the history of Spain was one long and uninterrupted success. Portugal, Navarre, Roussillon were annexed; she acquired Artois, Franche Comté, the Netherlands, the Milanese, Naples, Sicily, Sardinia, the Balearic Islands, the Canaries. One of her kings was emperor of Germany; another married and influenced a queen of England. The Turks were broken and beaten back, France was humbled, a king of France was captured and led prisoner to Madrid. In America, Africa, Asia, the Philippines, their conquests were impressive. Her military spirit was unequalled. Her eminent literary men, such as Calderon, Cervantes, Lope de Vega, and a score more, were military men. The combination was the admiration and terror of Europe.

Such a force, headed by able men, succeeds; when incompetent leaders come, it is sure to decay. Incapable hereditary rulers come, and deterioration begins. This is in strong contrast to England, where imbecilic and criminal kings have been unable to stay national progress. In Spain, when government slackened, the nation fell to pieces. After the great sovereigns came Philip III and Philip IV, idle, ignorant, low debauchees. Charles II, last of the distinguished Austrian line, was in every way ridiculous and contemptible. At thirty-five, he was completely bald, paralyzed, epileptic, notoriously impotent. In appearance he was a drivelling idiot. He was foul with superstition, being unwilling to sleep without the presence of his confessor and two friars, to chase away his personal devil. With such little princes, Spain became utterly debased, insulted with impunity, stripped of her best possessions, wholly degraded.

The Clergy Ruin Spain.—The increasing influence of the Spanish church was the first consequence of the decline of the government. Listless Philip III ceased to directly superintend the government, as his predecessors had done, and entrusted the power to Lerma. This change weakened the excutive, in the eyes of the people; and Lerma, realizing this, formed a still closer alliance with the clergy. As a result, convents and churches multiplied with alarming speed. The Cortes, the national legislative body, ventured to protest, in 1626, against this condition; pointing out that not a day passed in which some layman was not robbed to enrich the church, and that there were now more than 9,000 monasteries in Spain, in addition to the nunneries. Before the death of Philip III, the number of clergy performing in the Cathedral of Seville had swelled to one hundred; there were 14,000 chaplains in the diocese of Seville, 18,000 in Calahorra. The richer the church became, the more eagerly the laymen desired to enter it. In the rest of Europe, a great secular literature was com-

mencing; in Spain, the clergy monopolized this field still.
Cervantes, three years before his death, became a Franciscan
monk. Lope de Vega was a priest, and an officer of the Inquisition, assisting in 1623 in an auto da fe, or public burning.
Calderon was chaplain to Philip IV, and has been called the
poet of the Inquisition, so fanatical are his sentiments. This
is true of all other distinguished writers of the time.

In such a society, anything approaching a scientific spirit
was impossible. Whatever concerned the church was treated
with timid veneration. Thousands of volumes were written to
prove the necessity of religious persecution, in a country where
not one man in a thousand doubted the propriety of burning
heretics. Saints were in great repute, and their biographies
were written in profusion. It was the influence of the clergy,
in the reign of Philip III, which caused the expulsion of the
Moor, under circumstances of horrid barbarity. By torture,
burning, and threats all the Moors had been, superficially at
least, converted to Christianity, by 1526. Being baptized,
they were now subject to the church, which gave them the
most barbarous treatment. They were ordered to abandon
everything which could possibly remind them of their former
religion. They must learn Spanish, give up their Arabic books,
neither read or write Arabic, or speak it in their own homes.
They were to abandon amusements and even clothes which
their fathers had known. Their women must go unveiled;
and, as bathing was a heathenish custom, both public and
private baths were to be destroyed.

At length the Moriscoes, or converted Moors, were goaded
into rebellion. In 1568 they defied the Spanish monarchy, a
contest lasting three years. In 1602, after years of partial
toleration under Philip II, the Archbishop of Valencia, backed
by the other clergy, presented a memorial to Philip III, blam-
ing the lack of faith of the Moriscoes for the disasters which
had befallen Spain. The king was urged to root out the converted Moors, as Saul had extirpated the Amelekites, and
David the Philistines. The Armada had failed, he said, because God would not let a land prosper which permitted

heretics at home; the recent expedition to Algiers had lost for
the same reason. He urged the king to exile all the Moriscoes,
except those condemned to work in the galleys, or slave in
the mines in America. The Archbishop of Toledo aided this,
saying that, rather than have the unbelievers corrupt the land,
he would have all of them, men, women and children, put to
the sword. A large party favored this: Bleda, the Dominican,
wanted every Morisco in Spain to have his throat cut, since
it was impossible to tell which were Christians, and God,
knowing his own, could reward in the next world those who
were really Catholics. In 1609, Lerma announced to the king
that the expulsion of the Moriscoes had become necessary.
"The resolution," replied Philip, "is a great one; let it be
executed." It was executed with unflinching barbarity. About
a million of the most industrious inhabitants of Spain were
hunted out like wild beasts, because their religious sincerity
was doubted. Many were slain, as they approached the coast;
others were beaten and plundered; the majority, in wretched
plight, sailed for Africa. During the passage, the crew, in
many of the ships, rose upon them, butchered the men, threw
the children into the sea, raped the women. Those who
landed were attacked by the Berbers, and many put to the
sword. How many perished is unknown: but it is said that,
of one expedition of 140,000 about 100,000 met frightful
death within a few months of their expulsion.

Now Spain was at last freed of pollution: and it was believed that all prosperity would follow. From nearly every
part of Spain the more industrious farmers and artisans had
been suddenly withdrawn. The cultivation of rice, cotton,
sugar, the manufacture of silk and paper, was destroyed at a
blow, much of it for ever. Spanish Catholics considered labor
beneath their dignity: to fight for the king, or enter the
church, were the only vocations worthy of a Spaniard. Arts
and manufactures, with the Moriscoes gone, degenerated, or
were entirely lost; immense stretches of land were left uncultivated. The solitudes gave refuge to smugglers and
brigands, and organized bands of robbers, which no subse-

quent government has entirely eradicated, became common. Worst of all, the victory made the church stronger. The minds of men succumbed, and remained prostrate. While the rest of Europe advanced, Spain remained stagnant. At the beginning of the 17th century, the population of Madrid was 400,000; at the beginning of the 18th century, it had sunk to 200,000. Seville, in the 16th century, had upward of 16,000 looms, employing 130,000 people; by the reign of Philip V, these looms had dwindled away to less than 300; in 1662, the population of Seville was less than one fourth of its former inhabitants. Toledo, in 1550, had fifty woolen manufactories; in 1665, it had thirteen. The art of manufacturing silk, for which Toledo was famous, was entirely lost, and 40,000 persons dependent on it lost their means of support. City after city dwindled, became inactive industrially. In the villages near Madrid, the inhabitants starved; and farmers refused to sell their food, lest their own families starve. In 1664, the President of Castile, with an armed force and the public executioner, went forth to force the farmers to bring produce to Madrid. The taxes could not be paid; tax-gatherers not only seized the beds and all the furniture, but actually unroofed the houses, and sold the materials of the roof for whatever they would bring. The inhabitants were forced to fly; the fields were left uncultivated; multitudes died from want and exposure; entire villages were deserted; upwards of two thirds of the houses were, by the end of the 17th century, entirely destroyed.

The spirit and energy of Spain died. The defeat at Rocroy in 1643 broke the military reputation of Spain. In 1656, it was proposed to fit out a fleet; there were no sailors left to man it. The charts had been lost, the pilots were notoriously ignorant. Late in the 17th century, most of the troops had deserted, and the few left were clothed in rags, received no pay, and were dying of hunger. The inhabitants of Madrid were starving to death. In 1680, workmen and traders organized themselves into armed bands, robbed, murdered, and pillaged in the light of day. For the next twenty years, the capital was ruled by anarchy. The police disbanded, and gave themselves up to rapine. The treasury was empty. In 1693, payment on all pensions was stopped, and crown officials mulcted of one third of their salaries. If this had continued for another generation, anarchy would have become permanent, and society broken up.

Effect of Foreign Influence.—Fortunately, in 1700, Charles II, the idiot king, died; and Philip V, a Bourbon, grandson of Louis XIV, received the throne, which he held for forty-six years. He was a Frenchman, by birth, education, feeling, and habits. After he ascended the throne, he neglected the Spaniards, and threw the power into the hands of his own countrymen. Spain became literally a province of France; all important matters were decided in Paris, and Philip received his orders from there. As early as 1682, Charles II had been obliged to entrust the military defense of the Spanish Netherlands to De Grana, the Austrian ambassador at Madrid. In 1704, the Duke of Berwick, an Englishman, commanded Spanish soldiers against the enemy; and, when the king removed him, he appointed Marshal Tessé, a Frenchman, in his place. Later Berwick was summoned to Madrid, and set to the defense of Estremadura and Castile. In 1707, he won the battle of Almansa, overthrowing the invaders, ruining the party of the pretender Charles, and making the seat of Philip secure. In 1710, Philip wrote to Paris, asking that the Duke de Vendôme be sent him as a general. English and French generals led all the Spanish troops.

In 1701, at Philip's request, the Frenchman Orry was sent to manage the finances. The second marriage of Philip in 1714, and the death of Louis XIV in 1715, weakened the French influence, and for a time almost destroyed it. Other foreigners came in. Between 1714 and 1726, the two most powerful men in Spain were Alberoni, an Italian, and Ripperda, a Dutchman. When Ripperda was dismissed in 1726, Koenigsegg, a German, took control. The national spirit in Spain had so died away that no native was capable of government. Under foreign leadership, the government began to show some signs of vigor. Some effort was made to shake the power of the clergy. In 1707, the clergy were forced to contribute a small sum to the support of government; in 1717, they were taxed more stringently, and priests who refused to pay were jailed or exiled. In spite of Spanish feeling against heretics, Alberoni concluded a treaty with Moslems, and supplied them with arms and money. He and the other officials were of course isolated from the mass of Spanish people. Gramont, writing during the latter half of the 17th century, pointed out that the upper classes were not only ignorant of science and literature, but knew not even the commonest things occurring in their country. Men of high position did not think it necessary that their sons should study; in any case, there were neither schools nor teachers. Books, except books of devotion, were esteemed as worthless; until the 18th century, Madrid had no public library. De Torres wrote that he had studied at the University of Salamanca for five years, before he heard that such things as the mathematical sciences existed. As late as 1771, the same university refused to allow the discoveries of Newton to be taught: since the system of Newton was not consistent with revealed religion, as that of Aristotle was. The Duke de Saint Simon, French ambassador to Madrid, remarked that, in Spain, science is a crime, and ignorance a virtue.

When, in 1760, it was proposed that the streets of Madrid be cleansed, this excited general anger. Vulgar and educated alike censured the plan. The medical profession were called on for their opinion; they had no doubt that the dirt ought to remain. To remove it was a new experiment; it was impossible to foresee the results of new experiments. Their fathers had lived in the midst of the dirt; why should not they do the same? Even the smell, of which some complained, was probably wholesome. For, the air being sharp and piercing, bad smells made the air heavy, and deprived it of injurious properties. The filth had best remain. Medical science had only two remedies: to bleed, and to purge. It was almost certain death to submit to Spanish medical treatment for any length of time. Philip V did not dare trust himself to Spanish doctors, but had an Irishman for his physician. Medicine was supplied from abroad; the most to hope from a pharmacy in a small town, was that its medicines were not poisons. In 1750, Spain did not possess one practical chemist.

Ensenada, the well-known minister of Ferdinand VI, tried to improve conditions. He pointed out that there was in Spain no professorship of public law, or of physics, or of anatomy, or of botany. There were no good maps of Spain; the best available came from France and Holland, but these were inaccurate. Foreign aid was called in: Cevi established the medical societies of Madrid and Seville, Virgili founded the college of surgery at Cadiz, and Bowles sought to awaken the Spaniards to the study of mineralogy. Linnaeus was asked to send a botanist from Sweden. But this movement came from the government, not from the people, and was useless. The people, being unable to doubt, were unwilling to inquire. In the 17th century, the Spanish nation fell into a sleep, from which, as a nation, it has never since awakened. Even the fine arts fell into decay; the mechanical arts were as depressed. No one could build a ship, or repair one. After 1752, the government secured O'Reilly, an Irishman, to remodel the infantry; Colonel Godin, a Frenchman, to head a naval academy at Cadiz; Maritz, a Frenchman, to improve the artillery; and Gazola, an Italian, to renovate the arsenals.

The mines, a great natural source of wealth, were either abandoned, or worked by other nations. The Germans worked the cobalt-mine in the valley of Gistau in Aragon; the silver mines of Guadalcanal, the richest in Spain, were undertaken by foreigners. The mercury mine of Almadén in La Mancha had ceased to produce profit; the Irish naturalist Bowles was commissioned to report on this, and showed that the miners sank their shafts perpendicularly, instead of following the direction of the vein. The government ordered the change made; the Spanish miners refused to mine other than their fathers had done. The mines had to be turned over to German laborers, under an Irish superintendent, to prosper at all. Similarly, Ripperda established a woolen manufactory at Segovia; but he had to import manufacturers from Holland. In 1757, Wall, then minister, constructed a larger manufactory at Guadalajara in New Castile; when its machinery went wrong, it was necessary to send to England for a workman to put it to rights. The advisers of Charles III at last invited thousands of foreign artisans to settle in Spain: even this was hopeless, to reawaken the sluggish Spaniards. A national bank was formed; but this, proposed by a Dutchman, and organized by a Frenchman, was not suited to backward Spain.

In diplomacy, the ablest men were foreigners. French influence secured the expulsion of the Jesuits in 1767; the Inquisition trembled, for fear it would be next. The anti-theological policy of Grimaldi was carried on after 1777 by Florida Blanca, his creature. He concluded a treaty with heretical Turkey, with Tripoli, Algiers, Tunis. Yet such liberal acts produced no lasting benefit, because of the abiding ignorance of the people, and their credulity. These treaties put an end to piratical attacks by Moslem corsairs, and seemed to promise a renewal of national prosperity. Charles III, who ruled 1759-1788, was an able ruler, with a definite anti-theological policy. Yet the attacks of his ministers, in assailing evils the people loved, increased popular love for the evils. The opinion must be altered, before the evil can be attacked. Such countries as France and Germany still believe that government can regenerate society; England has something of the same opinion, but is still too wise to enact any law of which the nation disapproves. Charles III found Spain a third-rate power, and left it a first-rate one. American colonies were decently treated, in contrast to England's contemporary tyranny; prosperity definitely commenced. Taxes, especially on the lower ranks and industry, were repealed. The literary and scientific classes were encouraged and protected. The power of the Inquisition was lessened. Schools were founded, colleges endowed, professors rewarded.

Madrid was so beautified by the king, that forty years after his death it was said that all the city's beauty was due to him. Roads were laid down, canals dug; the bandit-ridden Sierra Morena was filled with six thousand Dutch and Flemish settlers.

The death of Charles III ended all this. It became clear that these great works were not national, but political. It may be doubted "if such vast and uninterrupted progress has ever been seen in any country either before or since" as the ninety years progress from Philip V to the death of Charles III. Those who believe that a government can civilize a nation, and that legislators are the cause of social progress, will naturally expect that Spain reaped permanent benefit from these liberal maxims, thus put into execution. No reform can produce real good, unless it is the work of public opinion, and unless the people themselves take the initiative. The reaction came in Spain. In 1788 Charles IV succeeded to the throne, a king of the true Spanish breed, devout, orthodox, and ignorant. A weak and contemptible prince, his reactionary principles were so fully supported by the Spanish people, that in five years he had completely reversed the liberal policies it had taken three generations of statesmen to build up. The power of the church was restored; free discussion was absolutely forbidden; literary men were intimidated, and literature discouraged; the Inquisition was re-empowered, and awoke to fresh energy. The liberal ministers of Charles III were removed, some being banished or jailed. Darkness once more covered the face of Spain.

The French invasion quickly followed; and Spain tasted every calamity and degradation: calamity, which others may inflict, and degradation, which only a people itself can cause. During the present century, Spain has remained prostrate. There have been reaches toward the light. 1812, 1820, 1836 saw attempts to secure liberty and a free constitution: but, since the people did not demand these things, temporary successes were useless. Yet Spain had had municipal privileges and franchises even before England. We had no popular representation till 1264; in Castile, they had it in 1169, and in Aragon in 1133. The earliest charter granted to an English town was in the 12th century; Leon received a charter in 1020. Yet this originated as policy on the part of rulers, rather than in answer to demands from the people. When Charles IV favored the church, and discouraged free inquiry, he merely sanctioned those national habits which his predecessors had disregarded. The year after the Jesuits were expelled, the citizens of Madrid asked, as their annual favor of the king, that the Jesuits be allowed to return, and wear their usual dress, that Spain might be gladdened by the sight of these holy men.

What can you do with a nation like this? What is the use of laws, when the current of public opinion thus sets in against them? In the face of this, liberal government is powerless. Even the Inquisition, the most barbarous institution devised by man, was supported by the people. This grew out of superstition; and the only remedy for superstition is knowledge. The Spaniards possessed every good thing except knowledge. Their abounding gifts have availed them nothing, and will avail them nothing, as long as they remain ignorant. Education still remains in the hands of the clergy. The Inquisition, though finally abolished in 1820, still lives in spirit. The monasteries were suppressed; but they soon returned. A liberal movement in 1836 again crippled the clergy; in 1845, their restoration began; broken again by liberal ministers, and again restored in 1857. Under the high-sounding names of loyalty and religion lurk deadly evils, especially the evil of reverence. This is the sole national vice of Spain, and it has ruined Spain. Spain has never had a revolution, a grand national rebellion. The people, though often lawless, are never free. Even while they resist, the people revere. Their reverence for antiquity has robbed them of energy, buoyancy, and hope. While the world progresses, Spain sleeps on, untroubled, unheeding, impassive, receiving no impressions from the rest of the world, and making no impressions upon it. Democracy, monarchy, government by priests, government by municipalities, government by nobles, by representative bodies, by natives, by foreigners, have been tried, and tried in vain. Everything has been altered, except opinion: there has been every change, except a change in knowledge. Without these, all is hopeless.

CHAPTER IX

Scotland up to 1399.—In Scotland, the progress of the nation has been very slow, but, on the whole, very sure. The country is barren; the government has been almost invariably weak; the spirit of loyalty has been almost lacking, as far as kings were concerned. There have been more rebellions in Scotland than·in any other country, rebellions bloody as well as numerous. The Scotch have fought most of their kings, and slain many. Of a single dynasty, they murdered James I and James III, rebelled against James II and James VII, jailed James V, jailed and deposed Mary, jailed James VI, opposed Charles I. Three years before England rose against that prince, Scotland made war on him. When they captured him, they sold him to England—an unprecedented and striking thing. Yet, while in loyalty Spain differs from Scotland, in superstition the countries are alike. In both countries, intolerance has been and still is a crying evil; bigotry is constantly displayed, in spite of distinguished philosophers and men of learning.

This is the paradox of Scottish history. Knowledge has not produced the effects which have elsewhere followed it; a bold and inquisitive literature has not altered a grossly superstitious country; the people have opposed their kings, and succumbed to their clergy; they are liberal in politics, and illiberal in religion. Physical geography, as elsewhere, has influenced Scotch events. The location of Scotland exposed it to attacks of that nation of pirates which for years inhabited the Scandinavian peninsula. Natural obstacles divided the Highlands from the Lowlands; and made contact impossible until after 1750. The most fertile Scotch land is in the South,

99

exposed to English ravages. The accumulation of wealth was thus hindered; the growth of towns was discouraged; the municipal spirit could not develop.

The earliest fact we have concerning Scotch history, is the Roman invasion under Agricola, late in the 1st century. This made no permanent impression; even Severus, who made the last important expedition against Scotland in 209, did not penetrate beyond the Firth of Moray. At this time, the Romans themselves were deteriorating. Luxury, instead of refining them, corrupted them. In the world today, wealth is both the cause and the effect of progress, while poverty is the fruitful parent of weakness, of misery and of crime. When Rome ceased to be poor, she became vicious. Their empire gave them wealth, and wealth overthrew their empire. As Rome grew, it dwarfed. When Roman power loosened in Scotland, the Irish, or Scotti, as they were called, established themselves by force of arms in the west of Scotland, and collided with the Picts, who held the east. A struggle ensued, that lasted four centuries. In the middle of the 9th century, Kenneth McAlpine, king of the Scotti, compelled the Picts to surrender.

But the unified kingdom was to have no rest. Norway had become the greatest maritime power in Europe. That nation of pirates captured the Shetland Islands, then the Orkneys, and thus could conveniently pillage the coasts of Scotland. Another body took the Western Islands, crossed the channel, and settled in Western Ross. For three centuries their attacks prevented social improvement. The last great attack, under Haco of Norway in 1263, saw Scotland fall under fire and sword to the Norwegian, until the weather broke up the expedition, and scattered or destroyed the entire fleet. Conditions in Norway prevented further attacks; meanwhile, attacks from England began. By 1250, Norman and Saxon had become unified into a powerful nation, which naturally turned against its weaker neighbor on the north. In 1290 Edward I determined to avail himself of the confusion into which Scotland was thrown by disputes concerning the succession to the crown. In 1296 the sword was drawn, and Edward invaded. Before the war was over, millions had been squandered, and hundreds of thousands of lives lost.

During the long contest that followed, the Scotch, in spite of heroic resistance and occasional victories, had to endure every evil. The ambition of England was to subjugate the Scotch; and in this they failed. Yet the most fertile part of Scotland was prostrated by English ravages. In 1296, the English entered Berwick, the richest town in Scotland, destroyed the property, and slew most of the inhabitants. They marched on to Aberdeen and Elgin; the country was so desolated, that the Scotch could only fly to their mountain fastnesses, and wage from here a war similar to that their ancestors had conducted against Rome twelve centuries earlier. In 1298, the English burst in again, burnt Perth and St. Andrews, and ravaged south and west. In 1310, they invaded Scotland by the eastern boundary lands, and carried off such provisions that the Scotch were forced to feed on horses and carrion. In 1314 the Scotch rallied for the glorious victory of Bannockburn; yet Bruce, to baffle the invading English, had to lay waste all south of the Firth of Forth, in 1322. When Edward II reached Edinburgh, he plundered nothing, because there was nothing left to plunder. He did what he could; meeting with some convents, he fell upon them, robbed the monasteries of Melrose and Holyrood, burnt the abbey of Dryburgh, and slew those monks who, from age or disease, were unable to escape. In 1633 Edward III devastated the Lowlands, and much of the Highlands. In 1346, the English overran Tweeddale, the Merse, Ettrick, Annandale, and Galloway; in 1355, Edward burnt every church, every village, every town he approached. In 1385 Richard II traversed the southern counties to Aberdeen, spread destruction on every side, and burnt to ashes Edinburgh, Dumferline, Perth, and Dundee.

These disasters everywhere interrupted agriculture for several generations. Farming Scotland became a wilderness. The Scotch crept forth in the interims, built wretched huts, and tried to repair the ravages. But famine stalked abroad, and the horrid practice of cannibalism came in. A man and wife were brought to justice, for living for a considerable period on the bodies of children, whom they caught alive in traps, devouring their flesh, and drinking their blood. In the 15th century, devastations by the English became rare. Scotland drew breath again; but conditions had come in which could not be easily overcome. These were, the inordinate strength of the nobles, and the absence of the municipal spirit. The ravages of the English had caused these. This combination of events strengthened the power of the clergy. Thus everything is linked together; nothing is casual or accidental; the whole march of affairs is governed by general causes.

The first circumstance favoring the power of the nobles is the structure of the country. Mountains, fens, lakes, and morasses supplied the Scottish chieftains with retreats in which they could defy the crown. The war with England further loosened the authority of the crown. The crown properties lay south, and suffered especially from English raids. In 1346, David II fell into the hands of the English, and during his eleven years of captivity the nobles carried all before them, and affected the style and title of princes. In such a royal weakness, the natural allies of the crown would have been the citizens and free burgesses; but what towns had existed, had been destroyed in the raids. Peaceful industry became impossible anywhere in Scotland. During many centuries, there were no manufactures, and hardly any trade; business was conducted by barter. The Scotch had to import their arms, and even their ordinary agricultural implements. What towns there were, were small. Glasgow, founded about the 6th century, as late as the middle of the 15th century had only 1,500 persons, whose property consisted of some small cattle, and a few acres of poorly cultivated land. Dumferline, home of Scotch kings, in the 17th century, had only 1,000 citizens. Paisley, in 1700, had less than 3,000. Aberdeen, metropolis of the north, in 1592 had only 2,900 inhabitants. Rich Perth, the capital, in 1585 had under 9,000; Edinburgh, in the 14th century, had less than 16,000.

The general poverty made the citizens glad to purchase noble protection, by yielding up the little independence they had. The post of chief magistrate in the towns often became hereditary in some aristocratic family of the neighborhood. There was in Scotland no real popular representation. The so-called representatives were obliged to vote as they were ordered: they were, in reality, delegates of the aristocracy. In this situation, the king turned to the clergy. Yet the nobles were more than equal to the combination of king and clergy; though Scotland was already the seat of a large amount of superstition. In contrast to England, the scenery is immense and rugged, and inclines to superstition. The English witch was a miserable hag; in Scotland, she was a potent sorcerer, who mastered the evil spirit, and forced it to do her will. The long and dangerous wars further strengthened the clergy: at such times, the churches are filled, the priest speaks as the voice of God, and accounts for victories as his achievements, and losses as God's punishments. As the country became poorer, the spiritual classes became relatively richer. The wars drove people into the church, the sole place of safety. Moreover, farmers are more superstitious than industrial classes; and conditions in Scotland repressed manufacturing interests, as has been pointed out. Moreover, the wandering habits of barbarous times continued, which increased ignorance, and therefore increased the power of the clergy. No university was founded until the 15th century, that of St. Andrews in 1412. Up to the 14th century, no Scotch noble could sign his name. By the 15th century, due to these causes, the clergy had more power in Scotland than in any European power except Spain. The king joined with the clergy, and opposed the nobles; in 1560, this contest was brought to a close, by the triumph of the aristocracy, and the overthrow of the church. Yet the spiritual classes soon rallied, and, under the name of Protestants, became as formidable as they had been under the name of Catholics. When James VI of Scotland ascended the English throne, the power of the nobles began to decline, and that of the church to rise further. During the 17th and 18th centuries, this power was the chief obstacle to progress in Scotland. Moreover, as events developed, the Protestant movement in Scotland was not democratic, as elsewhere, but aristocratic. The Reformation, not being the work of the people, cherished its ancient pretensions, retained its ancient power, and sanctified superstition.

Scotland in the 15th and 16th Centuries.—Albany, regent from 1406 to 1419, strengthened the clergy, and struggled with the nobles. Backed by the church, Albany marched against the great chieftain Donald in 1411, forced him to renounce the earldom of Ross, and to give hostages. James I carried the policy on more vigorously. In 1425 the king arrested twenty of the principal nobles, put four to death, and confiscated several estates. Two years afterwards the king treacherously imprisoned more than forty chieftains at Inverness, and executed three. In these acts, the king exaggerated the power of political remedies. The legislator and the magistrate may, for a moment, palliate an evil; they can never work a cure. If every noble in Scotland had been put to death, and all their castles razed to the ground, their successors would nevertheless have been more influential than ever. The general loathing of tyranny makes it impossible that tyranny should ever finally succeed. The reaction against James I took place during his lifetime. In 1436 the nobles turned on him, and put him to death. To show his authority, the head of the Douglasses attended the marriage of James II, in 1449, with five thousand followers. It was discreditable, in this country, not to belong to a great clan; it was, in addition, highly unsafe. The Earls of Crawford and Ross in the north corresponded to Douglas in the south.

Yet the government continued to provoke these powerful forces. In 1440 the Earl of Douglas, a boy of fifteen, and his younger brother, were treacherously beheaded by the Scotch king. In 1452 the Earl of Douglas was openly murdered, in spite of a safe conduct with the royal signature, under the great seal. The ferocity of the Scotch character, a natural result of the ignorance and poverty of the people, permitted such acts to be done publicly. The crown, alienating itself from the nobles, welded itself more closely to the clergy. For twenty years the avowed confidential adviser of the king was Kennedy, bishop of St. Andrews, a bitter enemy of the nobles who had plundered him. There being no middle class, Scotland contained only government, clergy, and nobles; and the united first two, if they had succeeded, would have given Scotland the union of a despotic crown and a despotic church, the worst of all yokes.

Happily, the nobles were too strong to permit this. They seized James III, and jailed him; on his release, in 1488 they defeated him in the field, and put him to death. Under James IV, the same conditions continued. Under the advice of Elphinston, bishop of Aberdeen, the king, in 1508, revived obsolete statutes permitting him to take possession of noble estates and receive much of their property. During the reign of James V, the regent, Albany, twice threw up his power, and at last abandoned it altogether. The Douglasses seized the king; when he escaped, he threw the power of government into the hands of the church, which persecuted the nobles, and drove some of them from the country. They became outcasts, traitors, beggars. The struggle of nobles against church lasted thirty-two years, and ended in the triumph of the aristocracy, who in 1560 overthrew the church, and at one blow destroyed almost all of the Scotch hierarchy. James escaped in 1528, still a boy, under the influence of two archbishops, who were supreme. The Earl of Caithness was defeated and slain. Angus was driven out of Scotland, and his estates confiscated. The Earls of Bothwell, Home, Maxwell, the two Kerrs, and the barons of Buccleuch, Johnston, and Polwarth were jailed. In 1531, Crawford was deprived of his property, and Argyle imprisoned. The nobles remaining were treated coolly; the clergy filled all the offices. Judicial power was taken from the nobles, and given to the clergy.

This exasperated the nobles almost to madness. They threw themselves into the arms of Henry VIII of England, and leaned toward the Reformation. In Scotland, Protestants were bitterly persecuted; the clergy presented James with a list of three hundred nobles, whom they accused as heretics, and worthy of death. When James took the field against England, the nobles refused to follow: the king had to dismiss his army. The clergy sought to rally the forces; the English turned on the Scotch, and three hundred cavalry scattered ten thousand Scotch troops. The king's mind reeled; fever and stupor slowly killed him, in December 1542. The clergy fell in popular favor, because of this disgraceful war they had instigated. The nobles returned to Scotland, since Mary was still an infant. They had resolved to plunder the church; but they fell out as to how the spoils should be divided. In 1546 Beaton, the deposed archepiscopal guardian of Mary, was murdered by a young baron. The conspirators resolved to defend themselves. In this they were supported by John Knox, fearless, incorruptible, unrelenting, and frequently brutal. He openly justified the assassination; and, when they were captured, he was put to work in the galleys for two years.

Six years later, he returned to Scotland, and was eagerly welcomed by the nobles. He left Scotland the next year for Geneva, where he remained till 1559; by that time, the real struggle was over. Why he left is uncertain, unless it was an unwillingness to remain and play a subordinate part among the proud chiefs. In 1554 the queen dowager, Mary of Guise, became regent, relying on French troops to suppress the nobles. They now banded together as the Lords of the Congregation, and sent word to Knox to return, meanwhile organizing their forces. On May 11, 1559, he preached in Perth. After the sermon, a tumult arose, the people plundered the churches, and pulled down the monasteries. The queen marched with troops toward the town; the nobles faced her, and both sides agreed to disarm. Popular tumults broke out almost at once. The queen-regent had to retreat before the nobles, and, on June 29, the Protestants entered Edinburgh in triumph. In October, the queen-regent was formally deposed. In the winter, an English fleet sailed into the Firth, and anchored near Edinburgh, a tardy aid to the nobles. In January 1560, the Duke of Norfolk arrived at Berwick, and concluded a treaty in behalf of Elizabeth, by which the English army entered Scotland on April 2nd. Against this, the government could do nothing; and in July signed a capitulation, by which the French were to evacuate Scotland, and the lords to be supreme.

The speed of these events indicates the energy of the great forces controlling the whole movement. For a hundred and fifty years clergy and nobles had struggled; the result of the struggle was, the establishment of the Reformation, and the triumph of the nobles. All notion of apostolic succession, the imposition of hands, the divine right of ordination, were suddenly discarded. The offices of the church were performed by heretics, the majority of whom had not even been ordained. In 1560, every statute in favor of the church was revoked; and saying mass, or being present while it was said, was punishable by loss of goods, for the first offense; exile, for the second; and death, for the third. The institution had been supported by superstition; which can only be conquered by knowledge. The people were still excessively ignorant; therefore, their Protestantism remained superstitious.

The nobles now sought to plunder the church; but they had not counted upon the Protestant preachers. These demanded the church property; when it was refused, and the nobles turned on them, they threw themselves into the arms of the people. The Presbyterian clergy displayed a hatred of the upper classes. The Earl of Morton, made regent, hated the clergy beyond all bounds. Every year, the clergy became more democratic. Melville, who succeeded Knox, began to move secretly against the institution of bishops, which was too aristocratic to suit the popular mind. The First Book of Discipline, in 1560, was when the clergy were with the nobles; the Second Book, in 1578, showed them against the aristocracy, and hence against the institution of bishops. In 1582 the General Assembly appointed Melville Moderator. The church threatened Montgomery, a bishop elect, with excommunication; this threat caused his submission. At the time occurred the Raid of Ruthven, with the imprisonment of James VI for ten months. The clergy applauded the act; when the king was released, they insulted him to his face. They refused to offer up prayers for the king's mother Mary, now in Elizabeth's hands. In 1594, John Ross stated in the pulpit that king and advisers were all traitors. In 1596 David Black preached that the king of Scotland was Satan himself. Yet for all their faults, the clergy kept alive the spirit of national liberty. Then James VI became James I of England, and sought to conquer his clerical opponents with that vast power.

CHAPTER X

Scotland and the Bishops.—In December, 1596, a tumult arose in Edinburgh, which James determined to turn to his own uses. His plan was to turn into his own capital large bodies of armed and licensed bandits, who, by threatening to plunder the city, should force the clergy and citizenry to yield to whatever terms the king chose to dictate. He summoned Highland nobles and southern border barons, to bring their fierce retainers—men who lived by pillage, and whose delight was to plunge their hands in blood. Resistance was hopeless: the king proceeded, for the next three years, to establish the bishops, and rein the clergy. The king used, as an artifice, the method of packing the General Assembly with clergymen from the north of Scotland, where the old clan spirit flourished, instead of the democratic spirit. The General Assembly of 1600 met; but the king could not enforce his will. The most that the Assembly would grant was that the ecclesiastics might sit in parliament, but must yearly lay their commissions before the Assembly, and would be called, not bishops, but merely Commissioners of the Church.

In 1603, Elizabeth died, and the king of Scotland became also king of England. The next year the king dismissed a General Assembly, in an endeavor to show his power over it. In 1605, he again dismissed it, refusing to fix a date for its future meeting. Certain of the clergy met in despite of the king; whereupon he jailed fourteen, and indicted six for high treason, sentencing them to prison, and then perpetual exile. The king summoned Melville and seven colleagues to London, and there detained them, imprisoning Melville in the Tower.

In 1610, a General Assembly met at Glasgow, its members nominated by the crown. By their vote, the institution of bishops was re-established. The Scotch bishops had to travel to London, in order to be touched by some English bishops; the unworthy priests did this. They then deprived the towns of their privileges, and forced them to receive magistrates appointed by the bishops. They accumulated wealth, in the midst of universal poverty. They took command of the legislature, and enacted severe penalties against many of the clergy.

The reaction was preparing; as long as a country is sound, tyranny provokes rebellion, and despotism causes freedom. In 1637, the people rose. The riot broke out in Edinburgh; by October, the whole country was up. In November, 1638, the first General Assembly seen in Scotland for twenty years met in Glasgow. The Marquis of Hamilton, the king's commissioner, ordered them to disperse; they refused to obey, until they had done their work. The bishops were again abolished, and the democratic institution of presbyteries restored. Scarcely had the Scotch expelled their bishops, when they made war upon their king. In 1639, they took up arms against Charles I. In 1641, the king visited Scotland to appease them, and agreed to most of their demands. It was too late. Scotch and English united against the Stuart. As a last chance, the king threw himself upon the mercy of his northern subjects. But he had not only trampled upon their liberties, he had put them to enormous expense; and with true Scotch thrift, they sold him to the English, for a sum claimed as arrears for damages he had caused them.

After the execution of Charles I, the Scotch recognized his son as his successor. But first they made him sign a public declaration, expressing regret, and stating that his father had unjustly shed Scotch blood. He was required to keep a day of fasting and humiliation, with the whole nation praying for him, that he might escape the consequences of the sins of his family. The spirit thus displayed continued to animate the Scotch, fortunately for them. For, from 1660 to 1688, under Charles II and James II, they were again subjected to a tyranny so cruel and exhausting, that it would have broken the energy of almost any other nation. Parliament was forced to repeal all acts passed since 1633. The people, deserted by all but the clergy, were plundered, murdered, hunted like wild beasts. The bishops were restored, under cruel and rapacious Sharp. The jails overflowed, the victims were transported to Barbadoes and other unhealthy settlements. The people met for worship in private houses, in the fields: there, too, the bishops were upon them. A body of soldiers, commanded by Turner, a drunken and ferocious man, was let loose upon them. The sufferers, galled to madness, rose in arms. In some of the fairest parts of Scotland, fields were devastated, houses burned, men racked, women tortured and raped. Death was the penalty for preaching in the fields without permission. Lawyers bold enough to defend these were expelled from Edinburgh. In 1678, the Highlanders were brought down from their mountains, and during three months were encouraged to slay, plunder, and burn at their pleasure. Neither age nor sex were spared. The people were stripped naked, and sent out to die in the fields. Children, torn from their mothers, were foully abused in nameless ways; mothers and daughters were ravished and deflowered.

The nobles looked on in silence, lacking courage even to remonstrate. Parliament was equally servile. The people clung to the clergy, and the clergy to the people, and both were unchanged. The bishops formally addressed James II, calling him the darling of heaven, and hoping that God might give him the hearts of his subjects, and the necks of his enemies. James derived actual enjoyment from witnessing the agonies of his fellow-creatures—an abyss of wickedness, into which even the most corrupt natures rarely fall. Hideous tortures, breaking the bones of the leg, cruelly injuring the whole hand, were used. All the children in Annandale and Nithsdale, between the ages of six and ten, were torn from their parents, and threatened with immediate death. The adults were then banished to unhealthy settlements, many of the men losing their ears, and the women being branded on the hand or the cheek. Then William came in. The cause of the Stuarts was still espoused by the ravening Highlanders; and rebellions of 1715 and 1745 were their work. For all their crimes, let not the Highlanders be accused of the crime of loyalty: they were thieves and murderers, but not so foolish as to attach themselves to that degraded family, the Stuarts. This would have convicted the Highlanders of a species of insanity alien to their nature. The revolts of 1715 and 1745 were the last struggles in Great Britain of barbarism against civilization.

The Trading Spirit.—Toward the close of the 17th century, trading sprang up. By 1710, men began to leave off armor. The union of Scotland with England shrank the Scotch legislators into insignificance. The nobles ceased to love the country which could give them nothing; in return, the country ceased to love them. Some of the nobles joined the 1745 rebellion of the pretender, and were exiled with him. On their return after 1784, a fresh generation had grown up, which had forgotten them. Their right to try cases had been taken away in 1748. The 1707 union with England opened trade with America to Scotland. Greenock of its own initiative built a pier and capacious harbor, and rose from insignificance to high trading importance. The same causes drew Glasgow from obscurity. Linen manufacture was introduced here in 1725; Paisley dates from the same year. Trade became a common topic of discourse; ambitious men turned from the church to commerce, literature, and similar pursuits. Hence Scotland, in the 18th century, possessed for the first time an intellectual class and an industrial class. Statistics, scanty though they be, show this movement throughout Scotland, showing the existence of great general causes. Banking, canals prospered. A spirit of inquiry was abroad, great literature was produced. Yet the Scotch clung to their superstitions with singular tenacity.

In the moral world, as in the physical world, nothing is unnatural, nothing is strange. There are opposites, but there are no contradictions. It is the business of the historian to remove the popular ignorance on such subjects. His payment will not be high, in the accepted sense. Rewards, popular approval, the luxury of power, are not for him. Let him toil as he may, he will find, as the twilight of life approaches, that he must leave undone that he had vainly hoped to complete. "Once, I own, I thought otherwise. Once, when I first caught sight of the whole field of knowledge, and seemed, however dimly, to discern its various parts and the relations they bore to each other, I was so entranced with its surpassing beauty, that my judgment was beguiled, and I deemed myself able, not only to cover the surface, but also to master the details." In those early aspirations there may have been something fanciful, perhaps something foolish as well. Yet "such hopes belong to that joyous and sanguine period of life, when alone we are really happy; . . . when the affections are not yet blighted and nipped to the core; and when the bitterness of disappointment not having yet been felt, difficulties are unheeded, obstacles are unseen, ambition is a pleasure instead of a pang, and the blood coursing swiftly through the veins, the pulse beats high, while the heart throbs at the prospect of the future." Whatever is achieved, will be only a fragment of the original design.

CHAPTER XI

THE SCOTCH INTELLECT DURING THE 17TH CENTURY

The Scotch Clergy in Practice.—Scotland, then, presents the paradox of a people liberal in politics, and illiberal in religion; the brilliant, inquisitive, and sceptical literature of the 18th century was unable to weaken the superstition of the people. The operation of this superstition will be studied in the present chapter; and the final inquiry, concerning the philosophy of method, which alienated Scotch thinkers from the mass of the people, will be examined in the last chapter. After the latter part of the 16th century, every event in Scotland tended to strengthen the power of the clergy, by raising them up as the foremost defenders of their country. The war which the Scotch carried on against Charles I partook more of the nature of a crusade, than any ever waged by a Protestant country. Its main object was, to raise up presbyters, and to destroy bishops. The Scotch loved liberty, and hated England; yet these passions were mild, compared to their passion for their own Presbyterian polity. They fought for freedom, but more for religion. The 1643 union of England and Scotland was marked by the fact that the English wished a civil league; the Scotch, a religious covenant. As the Scotch insisted, the English had to give way.

The war was regarded as under the immediate protection of the Deity, on whose behalf it was carried on. It was a war for God, and for God's church, in the language of the times. Victory came, not from a general's skill, or an army's valor, but as an answer to prayer. When a battle was lost, it was because God was vexed at the people's sins, or desired to rebuke their trust in arms of flesh. Nothing was natural; everything was supernatural. To assist the Scots, winds were changed, storms lulled. The clergy were supreme; war, trade, literature, science, art, were held of no account unless they ministered to religion. Clergy and people were united against oppression; and the clergy, for upwards of a century, by their exertions stopped all intellectual culture, discouraged all independent inquiry, made men in religion fearful and austere, and darkened the whole national character.

During the 17th century, the Scotch passed the greater part of their time in what were called religious exercises. The sermons were so long and so frequent, that they absorbed all leisure; and the people never tired of hearing them. There was no limit to a preacher's wordiness, except his strength. Two hours of vehement preaching was about the limit of the ordinary clergyman, for the time must be marked by excessive toil and sweat; a man like Forbes thought nothing of preaching for five or six hours. Since such men were rare, relays of preachers were present in the same church, who replaced each other when breath and vigor gave out. By the middle of the century, the people had come to look upon their preacher as a god, and to treasure every word that fell from his lips. Their power of endurance was marvelous: a congregation would remain for ten hours, listening to sermons and prayers, interspersed with singing and readings. In 1670, in a single church in Edinburgh, thirty sermons were delivered each week. In 1653, when the sacrament was administered, the congregation fasted on Wednesday; and listened to eight hours of prayers and sermons; on Saturday, they heard two or three sermons; on Sunday, at times the service lasted twelve hours; and three or four additional sermons were preached on Monday, by way of thanksgiving.

The parish clergyman selected certain laymen to be his elders; they, assembled together, formed the Kirk Session, and this little court was far more powerful than any civil tribunal. By its aid, the minister became supreme. Whoever presumed to disobey him was excommunicated, deprived of his property, and condemned to eternal hell. Each quarter of the parish had the minister's spy; private houses were searched and ransacked to see if any one was absent from church while the minister was preaching. To him, all must listen, all must obey. Without the consent of his tribunal, no person might engage himself as a domestic servant or field laborer. To pass the preacher on the street without saluting him was a crime. His very name was sacred, not to be taken in vain. The clergy told their hearers that whatever was said from the pulpit was binding upon all believers, and was to be regarded as proceeding immediately from the Deity. They claimed the power, not only of foretelling man's future state, but of controlling it: by their judgments they could open and shut the gates of heaven or hell. Moreover, their word could hasten a sinner's death, and cut him off in his prime to respond at once before the judicial bench of God.

It was told how a Catholic, who made faces at a Presbyterian minister, died immediately in his presence. A minister named Hog was laughed at by a scoffer, who died that same night. A minister named Semple had a mannerism of putting out his tongue; when this excited the mirth of a drunkard, who stuck out his own tongue, the latter's tongue could not be withdrawn, and the man died in a few days. A woman who scolded the divine Peden was cursed at once with a sore tongue. Three gentlemen quietly left church during a sermon: one broke his neck by falling from a horse, another was found with his throat cut, the third died a violent death also. The Laird of Hilton once pulled a clergyman out of a pulpit into which the religious man had unlawfully intruded. "For the injury you have done to the servant of God," cried the enraged preacher, "you shall be brought into this church like a sticked sow." Soon after, the lord was stabbed in a quarrel, and, still bleeding, was brought into the very church. A young girl laughed at Peden; for this, he denounced against her the judgment of God, and she was drowned soon thereafter, with the aid of a wind from God, which blew her into the sea. A trader refused to aid a pecuniarily embarrassed minister, and was denounced for it. His business declined, and he died an idiot; both his sons went mad, as did a daughter; the other daughter's husband became destitute, and the children of the marriage became beggars, so that the heinous crime might be visited to the third generation.

To sue a minister in court would provoke equally frightful calamities, as well attested cases established. The clergy, thus made arrogant, would not allow a stranger to be in the parish, without listening to their sermons. They were hardly modest as to their own abilities: they stated that they had their instruction straight from heaven; that they were Christ's ambassadors; that they were rightly termed angels. No one had a right to refuse obedience to them. They were the joy and delight of the earth. They were musicians, singing the song of sweetness; nay, they were sirens, who sought to allure men from the evil path, and save them from perishing. They were chosen arrows, stored up in the quiver of God. They were burning lights and shining torches. They were properly called stars, expressing the eminence of their office, and its superiority over all others. At the death of a clergyman, a star was miraculously exhibited in the heavens, and was seen by many persons, although it was midday. Whenever a Scotch minister died, signs and omens appeared. The candles would be mysteriously extinguished, without any wind or any human touch; the appearance of a supernatural animal, as a rat, would be God's message that the minister's life would soon cease. For years the clergyman's body would remain unchanged and undecayed. A minister was miraculously watched over and protected in this world. Angels peculiarly favored him; it was well known that the celebrated Rutherford, when only four years old, having fallen into a well, was pulled out by an angel, who came there to save his life. Another clergyman, who overslept, was roused to his duty by three strange knocks, that never failed on Sundays or communion days; and ceased only when he became old and infirm.

The National Character Mutilated.—These and similar stories filled the Scotch mind with a belief in miraculous interferences, only to be paralleled in the monkish legends of the middle ages. Their success in corrupting the national intellect is less well known. The Scotch hardness and moroseness of character, the want of gaiety, the indifference to the enjoyments of life, are traceable to the same source. The strongest clerical weapon was the doctrine concerning evil spirits and future punishment. It was generally believed that the world was overrun by evil spirits, who went up and down the earth, lived in the air, and made luring mankind their business. Satan was their head; visiting the earth as a black dog, a raven, a bull, a white man in black clothes, a black man in black clothes, with ghastly face, no shoes, and one cloven foot. He had lived already for more than 5,000 years; his cunning increased constantly. He could and did seize men and women, and carry them off through the air. At times he had impudently attired himself as a clergyman. He constantly tempted the clergy, who, of course, never yielded; but most laymen did. He could raise tempests, and affect men's bodies; could turn them to suicide and murder. Yet the Christian had not had a full religious experience who had not literally seen Satan, talked to him, and fought with him.

The consequence of this was that the people became almost crazed with fear. When Satan's name was mentioned, the church would resound with signs and groans of consternation. The people listened with gasping breath, and with hair standing on end. The images of terror persisted: people believed that the devil was always at hand; a sudden noise, even the sight of a stone, would revive the associations, and bring back the language heard from the pulpit. To excite fear was the paramount object of the clergy. In their eyes, God was not a beneficent being, but a cruel and remorseless tyrant. All mankind but a limited few were doomed to eternal misery. Hell was full of great fires, to roast the wicked, hanging up in the flames by their tongues. They would be lashed with scorpions, and see their companions writhing and howling around them. Burning oil and scalding lead, a river of fire and brimstone wider than the earth, were ready for them: their bones, lungs and liver would boil, but never be consumed. Worms were to prey upon them, and devils jeer at their pains. One hell would be succeeded by another, with fresh agonies in each place—all the work of God and of the Scotch clergy. God had prepared this hell before men were created, to be ready for man's reception. In latter days, hell had been enlarged.

To God, the clergy ascribed revenge, cunning, a constant disposition to inflict pain. In his insane anger, God raged against walls and houses and senseless creatures, wreaking His fury and scattering desolation on every side. If a country starved, God was smiting it for its sins. All this drove out of the Scotch character hope, and love, and gratitude. A fire, a boil, the smallpox, were God's petty snipings at man. Earthquake, comet, eclipse, were his warnings. Nearly every act on earth was sinful. All natural affections, all social pleasures, all amusements, all the joyous instincts of the human heart were evil, and were to be rooted out. It was sinful for a mother to wish to have sons; if she had any it was sinful for her to wish for their welfare. It was a sin to please yourself, or to please others. All pleasures, however slight, were to be carefully avoided. We should attempt to edify a company, but never to amuse it. Cheerfulness, especially when it rose to laughter, was to be guarded against; our associates should be grave and sorrowful men. It was a sin to smile on Sunday. Even on weekdays, the religious hardly ever smiled, but sighed, groaned, and wept. A true Christian would be careful, in his movements, to preserve invariable gravity, never running, but walking soberly, and not stepping briskly, as unbelievers do. It was wrong to take pleasure in beautiful scenery. Nature's energy had already departed; she was worn out and decrepit; she would soon perish. Owing to the sin of man, all things were getting worse, and nature degenerating, so that lilies were losing their whiteness, and roses their smell. The heavens were aging, the

sun growing feeble. The world afforded nothing worth looking at, except the Scotch Kirk, incomparably the most beautiful thing under heaven. To write poetry, to listen to music,
to dance, to celebrate New Year's Eve, to be happy at a
christening, to make merry at marriages, were all evil.

Everything man did was sinful, no matter how pure his
motives. Man was now inferior to the beasts that perish.
One of the worst crimes was teaching children new words—
a horrible custom, justly visited by divine wrath. The clergy
formed little lawmaking bodies, which all must obey. It was
a sin for a Scotchman to travel in a Catholic country, or for
a Scotch innkeeper to admit a Catholic into his inn. It was
a sin for a Scotch town to hold market on Saturday or Monday, since both were near Sunday. It was a sin for a Scotch
woman to wait at a tavern; or for her to live alone; or for
her to live with her unmarried sisters. It was a sin to go
from town to town on Sunday, no matter how pressing the
business might be. It was sinful to have your garden watered
or your beard shaved on Sunday: horse-exercising, walking in
the fields, enjoying the fine weather by sitting at the door of
your own house, were all wicked on the Lord's day. Bathing
was a very grievous offense; no man should go swimming on
Sunday. It was a sin to cleanse one's body: the great object
of life was to be in a state of constant affliction. Men should
not enjoy their meals, or make money, or save it. To be poor,
dirty, hungry, to pass through life in misery, and leave it with
fear, to be plagued with boils, and sores, and diseases of every
kind, to be always sighing and groaning, these were proofs of
goodness. The people's faces soured, and grew downcast. The
national character of the Scotch was dwarfed and mutilated.

The clergy to-day have weakened; they have ceased to use
the language of power, and have been forced to compromise.
Yet they still attack pleasures, wealth, and the love of money:
although "no one passion . . . has done so much good to
mankind as the love of money." Without it, man would re-
lapse into barbarism. Protestants hold that only the Catholic
church goes into anti-human extravagances; that is a mis-

take. Wherever a class has great power, it exhibits tyranny. The Scotch Protestants went beyond any section of the Catholics, except the Spanish. They sought to destroy both human pleasures and human affections. It was sinful to save a ship on Sunday: better let men drown than break the Sabbath. They taught the father to smite his unbelieving child, and to slay his own boy rather than allow him to propagate error. They laid their rude hands on "the holiest passion of which our nature is capable, the love of a mother for her son." When the Scotch Kirk was at the height of its detestable power we find nothing in history to compare with it, except the Spanish Inquisition.

CHAPTER XII

THE SCOTCH INTELLECT DURING THE 18TH CENTURY

Through Adam Smith.—The practical boldness displayed in Scotland in the seventeenth century became, in the eighteenth, a speculative boldness. In nearly every other country, where the intellect has faced the church, the secular philosophy has been an inductive philosophy, rising from individual and specific experience. In this, experience precedes theory; by the deductive method, theory precedes experience. In theology, certain principles are taken for granted; since they may not be questioned, the only course remaining is to reason downward. The inductive method concedes nothing, but insists on reasoning upward, demanding that man have the right of ascertaining his principles for himself. In a complete method, the two methods will be supplementary, and not antagonistic.

Scotland, being essentially theological, followed the theological or deductive plan. Sermons and theological writings are essentially deductive; no divine attempted an inductive argument. They proceeded from generals to particulars, instead of from particulars to generals. The inductive or analytic spirit being thus unknown, and the deductive or synthetic spirit alone being favored, it happened that the great intellectual movement of the eighteenth century found the deductive method ready at hand. The inductive method did not influence Scotch philosophers at all.

The beginning of Scotch secular philosophy is due to Francis Hutcheson. Born in Ireland, of Scotch family, he was educated at Glasgow, and in 1729 was appointed professor of philosophy there. Hutcheson strenuously advocated that right of private judgment which the Scotch Kirk had not only assailed, but had almost destroyed. Every one must judge according to his own lights. Such a large view of liberty was far in advance of the country in which it was propounded, and could only influence a few thinking men. In place of the element of faith, Hutcheson introduced inquiry, discussion, and doubt. He held that the emotions which beauty excites were not sinful, but were good in themselves, and were entitled to scientific investigation. In every way he endeavored to break down that gloomy spirit the clerics had instilled. He declared that the fine arts were to be cherished, that wealth was beneficial, and that man's natural appetites are lawful and highly virtuous. In his eyes, they were virtuous because they were natural.

Hutcheson assumed that all men have what he terms a moral faculty, which, being an original principle, does not admit of analysis. He further assumed that the business of this faculty is to regulate all our powers. From these two assumptions he reasons downward to the visible facts of our conduct, and deductively constructs the general scheme of life. Hence, the judgments men pass upon the conduct of others, or of themselves, are, in their origin, altogether inexplicable; each judgment being merely a different form of one great moral faculty. Since that faculty escapes observation, the judgments must be deemed primary, and arguments may be constructed from them. Hutcheson believed that from a certain number of original principles, he could construct the theory and explain the march of human affairs, with little or no aid from the experiences of past or present.

The next great attempt to study the actions of men scientifically, and to generalize the principles of their conduct without the intervention of supernatural ideas, was made by Adam Smith, who, in 1759, published his *Theory of Moral Sentiments*, and, in 1776, his *Wealth of Nations*. To understand the philosophy of this greatest of all Scotch thinkers, both works must be taken together, and considered as one;

since they are, in reality, the two divisions of a single subject. In the first book, he investigates the sympathetic part of human nature; in the second its selfish part. All of us are both sympathetic and selfish. If Adam Smith had completely accomplished his vast design, he would at once have raised the study of human nature to a science, leaving nothing for further investigators but to ascertain the minor matters of affairs. Using the deductive method, he employed an artifice used in the inductive, wherever the materials of any investigation are numerous and complicated. That is, he made an imaginary separation of inseparable facts. A result arrived at in this way cannot be strictly true; but, if we have reasoned accurately, it will be as near truth as the premises from which we start. The separate inferences may eventually be coordinated into a single system, which will contain perfect truth.

Geometry exhibits the most perfect example of this logical stratagem. The object of the geometrician is, to generalize the laws of space; in others words, to ascertain the necessary and universal relations of its various parts. Inasmuch, however, as space would have no parts unless it were divided, the geometrician is forced to assume such a division; and he takes the simplest possible form of it, a division by lines. A line considered as a fact, that is, as found in the actual world, always has two qualities, length and breadth, however infinitesimal the breadth may be. The geometrician, baffled by this complication, by a scientific artifice strikes off one of these qualities, and asserts that a line is length without breadth. He knows that the assertion is false, but knows that it is necessary. The flaw is too minute to be perceived; but that there is a flaw, appears certain.

In the *Theory of Moral Sentiments*, Adam Smith lays down one great principle from which he reasons, and to which all the others are subordinate. That is, that the rules which we prescribe to ourselves, and which govern our conduct, are solely arrived at by observing the conduct of others. We judge ourselves, because we have previously judged them.

Our ideas are obtained from without, and not from within. Inasmuch as we can not directly know what others actually feel, we must in imagination put ourselves in their places. From this many social phenomena may be explained. We naturally sympathize with joy more than with sorrow. From this springs our admiration for prosperous persons, and indeed the ranks of social distinctions. Loyalty comes similarly from a sympathy with those above us. Custom and fashion, all of our criminal laws, the irritability of poets, the coolness of mathematicians, all illustrate the workings of sympathy.

By this bold stroke, Adam Smith excluded from the field of inquiry the primary principle selfishness, and admitted only its great antagonist, sympathy. He denied that sympathy is in any way a selfish principle. His next work ignored sympathy, and argued from selfishness. *The Wealth of Nations* assumed that selfishness is the main regulator of human affairs, as his previous work had assumed sympathy to be. This is "probably the most important book which has ever been written, whether we consider the amount of original thought which it contains, or its practical influence." Great as a proximate cause of legislation, his power came in part from the circumstances and forces of the time. The breadth of his treatment is tremendous, and the handling bold and masterly.

At the beginning of the study he lays down two propositions: (1) that all wealth is derived, not from land, but from labor; and (2) that the amount of wealth depends, partly on the skill with which the labor is conducted, and partly on the proportion between the number of those who labor, and those who do not labor. The rest of the book applies these principles to explain the growth and mechanism of society. He asserts throughout that the great moving force of all men, all interests, and all classes, in all ages and countries, is selfishness. Considering society as a whole, it nearly always happens that men, in promoting their own interests, will unintentionally promote the interests of others. The practical lesson is, not to restrain selfishness, but to enlighten it.

Man's tendency to better himself is so salutary and powerful, that it often procures the progress of society, in spite of the folly and extravagance of rulers. But for this selfishness improvement would be impossible. Human institutions constantly stop our advance, by thwarting our natural inclinations. In the book Adam Smith hardly admits humanity at all. Thus slaves were freed, because they were few in number, and, therefore, small in value. Different systems of morals are ascribed entirely to the power of selfishness. The laborer owes no gratitude to his master for wages, contrary to the established opinion; his labor, after all, produces all the wealth. Malthus's great work on population, published after the death of Adam Smith, would have been impossible, but for this earlier achievement. The hospitality of the monks of the middle ages Adam Smith attributes to the same cause, expressed in their excess of supplies received in kind, which could earn gratitude only by being spent in hospitality.

The Deductive Method Progresses.—A great contemporary of Adam Smith was David Hume, whose views respecting political economy were published in 1752. He lacked the comprehensiveness of Adam Smith; his polished style shows his lack of imagination. His *History of England* fails to make us sympathize with the bold and generous natures of the seventeenth century, who risked their all to preserve liberty. He ascribed the Great Rebellion to the spirit of party, and ridiculed all its leaders. In philosophy he saw that nothing could be done, except by a spirit of fearless and unrestrained liberty. But this was the liberty of his own class: the liberty of thinkers, not of actors.

Among his speculative views the most important are his theory of causation as discarding the idea of power, and his theory of the laws of association. His work on the principles of morals, by generalizing the laws of expediency, prepared the way for Bentham. In his economic theories, he advocated those principles of free trade, which politicians began to adopt many years after his death. He insisted that all commodities, though apparently bought by money, are in reality bought by labor. Money, therefore, is not the subject of commerce, and is of no use except to facilitate it. Hence, it is absurd for a nation to trouble itself about the balance of trade. The rate of interest does not depend upon the scarcity of metals, but upon larger causes. He detected the fundamental error of Adam Smith, in resolving price into wages, profit, and rent; whereas it is now known that price is a compound of wages and profit, and that rent is not an element of it, but a result of it. This discovery is the cornerstone of political economy.

It is noticeable that Hume and Adam Smith, who made such immense additions to our knowledge of the principles of trade, had no practical acquaintance with it. One of the capital defects of Hume's mind was his disregard of facts. He disregarded merely because he reverenced ideas. His method was deductive; if it had been inductive, rising from facts to generalizations, he could not have written one of his works, since political economy is as definitely a deductive science as is geometry. Adam Smith expressed a want of confidence in statistics. This was right, since statistics express both sympathy and selfishness, and he discarded sympathy in *The Wealth of Nations*. Finding statistics unmanageable he rejected them as part of his science, and used them merely by way of illustration.

The same determination to make ideas precede facts appears in Hume's *Natural History of Religion*. This is an admirable example of the deductive method. Hume believed that by observing the principles of human nature, as he found them in his own mind, it was possible to explain the whole course of moral and physical affairs. His object was to ascertain the origin and process of religious ideas; he arrives at the conclusion that the worship of many gods must everywhere precede the worship of one god. His reasoning is purely speculative. Cudworth, who wrote the *Intellectual System of the Universe* eighty years before, collected first the evidence, then pronounced his contrary judgment, that in the ancient world belief in one god prevailed. Reid in philosophy lacked wide knowledge, and possessed a natural timidity; he loved truth, not for itself, but for its practical results. He opposed Hume because the latter's bold speculations might unsettle men's opinions. Expediency, not truth, controlled him. He objected to Hume's deductive method; and then used the method himself, in the constructive part of his book. This is an excellent example of the potency of the national method of thought, in causing a man to adopt a method which he had rightly objected to.

In physical science the laws of heat occupy a prominent place. Our present knowledge of the laws of heat may be briefly stated as branching into five fundamental divisions: latent heat; specific heat; conduction of heat; radiation of heat, and, finally, the wave theory of heat, which is causing us to look upon heat as not matter, but a mere display of force. The indestructibility of force is now believed with the indestructibility of matter; and this emphasis upon the regular and compulsory march of physical affairs must ultimately influence other and higher departments of inquiry. The laws of latent heat and specific heat were discovered in Scotland. Soon after 1750 Black, professor at the University of Glasgow, turned his attention in this direction. He showed that when ice is turned into water the heat remains in the substance without raising its temperature; this he called latent or hidden heat. Black, it is true, regarded heat as matter, and not force. But this was a mere hypothesis bequeathed to him, for which he cannot be held responsible. His own efforts undermined the material theory of heat. His method was deductive, since the inductive would not have sufficed where the heat escaped the senses entirely. Black's intellect may be called deductive; it led him to the theory of the indestructibility of heat, which is connected with the doctrine of the indestructibility of force.

England's two mightiest intellects were Shakespeare and Newton; it was natural that Shakespeare should precede. Our poetry has lost its original marks of inspiration; the imagination has been reined by the discoveries of science, and the spirit which inspires them. We have lost much of our imagination; but knowledge has supplanted it. Leslie, in 1804, began to investigate heat also; and some of his views mark an epoch in science. Such was his generalization respecting the connection between the radiation of heat and its reflection: those which reflect it most radiating it least, those which radiate it most reflecting it least. It is true that he regarded heat as an elastic fluid; yet he saw that there was no fundamental difference between heat and light. His method, Leslie said, he secured from the poets, whom he had always noticed were consummate observers. Poetry's treasury of truths, he said, science must take advantage of. He saw that the divisions of nature have no existence, except in our minds; he was almost prepared to do away with that imaginary division between the organic and the inorganic world, which still troubles many of our physicists. "They, with their old notions of inanimate matter, are unable to see that all matter is living," and that what we term death is a mere expression by which we signify a fresh form of life.

Another expression of the Scotch deductive mind appears in the geologic speculations of Hutton, late in the eighteenth century. It is known that the two great forces which have altered the face of the earth have been fire and water; it is believed that the older rocks are chiefly the result of fusion by fire, and the later, of water deposit. William Smith, who established geology in England, did it by inductively studying the strata himself. In Germany, a country almost as deductive as Scotland, in 1787, three years before William Smith began his labors, Werner, by his work on the classification of the mountains, laid the foundation of the German school of geology. His influence was immense; but his method was on a chain of argument from cause to effect. He assumed that all the great changes through which the earth has passed were due to the action of water. According to his system, there was originally one vast and primeval sea, which, in course of time, deposited the primitive rocks. The base of all was granite; then gneiss; and others followed in their order. Agitations rose beneath the surface of the water, which destroyed part of the earlier deposits, and gave birth to new rocks, formed out of their ruins. The stratified thus succeeded to the unstratified, and something like variety was established. Another period came, in which the face of the water, instead of being merely agitated, was swept by tempests; life was generated, plants and animals sprang into existence. The sea gradually retired, and the foundation was laid for the epoch in which man entered the scene.

Erroneous though this• was in detail, it exerted a great influence. For the great enemy of knowledge is not error, but listlessness. This provoked a controversy, and out of the heat of discussion truth tends to emerge. The method adopted by Werner was deductive, since he argued from a supposed cause to the effects. Exactly the same process, on the same subject, and at the same time, was going on in Scotland. Hutton, founder of Scotch geology, published in 1788 his *Theory of the Earth,* using Werner's method, with no knowledge of Werner's activity. While Werner reasoned from the agency of water, Hutton reasoned from the agency of fire. Hutton lived in a country where many of the laws of heat had been generalized, and where inorganic physics had acquired a great reputation. From this difference, the followers of Werner are known as Neptunists, those of Hutton as Plutonists. In method they agreed. The truth probably includes both sets of results. Yet Hutton did valuable work in explaining the metamorphic rocks; showing their relationship to the sedimentary rocks above, and the igneous rocks below. In his speculations concerning subterraneous fires, he preferred to draw conclusions from ideas, rather than from inspecting any region of active volcanoes. In more than one instance Hutton reasoned from a theory to some fact, which subsequent experiment indicated was sound, although at the time it was regarded as revolutionary and contrary to all observation.

This study has not mentioned Watt and his invention of the steam-engine, because an invention is a lesser matter than a discovery. Watt's only discovery was of the composition of water; he was the first to discover that it was composed of two gases. While this has been important in chemistry, it has neither involved nor suggested any new law of nature, and has, therefore, no claim to mark an epoch in the history of the human mind. His method was different from that of Cavendish, the Englishman whose adherents dispute the claim of Watt. For Watt proceeded deductively, as might have been expected; and Cavendish inductively.

Cullen and John Hunter.—In organic science the Scotch labors were also remarkable. It is highly probable that there is no real difference between the organic and the inorganic worlds, the worlds of life and lifelessness. Nature has no gaps or chasms; all things flow into each other without break. The microscope has already shown us organisms invisible to the naked eye, which possess most of our organs and functions, and have a nervous system indicating pain and enjoyment. It has detected hidden life in the glaciers of Switzerland and the polar ice. For the present, however, this embracing idea must remain unproved.

When we turn to organic matter, investigations tend in two main directions: to study the normal workings of healthy animals, and to ascertain their laws in an unusual, unhealthy, or abnormal course. The first of these is called physiology; the second, pathology. Scotland produced in the eighteenth century two pathologists of great ability, Cullen and John Hunter. Hunter, in fact, was great as physiologist also. In 1751 Cullen was appointed professor of medicine in the University of Glasgow; in 1756, he was removed to the University of Edinburgh, where his celebrated lectures were delivered. He passed from physics to pathology, where he could indulge in that love of theory which was his ruling passion, and with an undue devotion to which he has been reproached.

In his eagerness to argue from principles to facts, instead of from facts to principles, Cullen laid down, in the most important of all arts, a method of procedure dangerous in the extreme. He said that, since theory and practice could not be separated in disease, it was unimportant which came first. This would permit theories to control observations. Nothing could explain this, except that Cullen lived in the country in which the deductive method was inevitable. As Adam Smith mutilated his phenomena by division, so did Cullen. It was obvious that the human frame consisted partly of solids and partly of liquids; and Cullen reasoned almost entirely from the laws of the solids, allowing the liquids to be only the indirect causes of diseases. This assumption, though false, was justifiable. Yet, as Adam Smith supplemented his study of sympathy by one of selfishness, it was incumbent on Cullen to supplement his study of solids by one of liquids. A union of the two theories might have raised a science of pathology, as complete as the then state of knowledge allowed. To do this his mind was not fitted; and his researches and theorizings stopped with that doctrine medical writers call Solidism.

According to Cullen, all the solids in the human body are either simple or vital. The simple solids retain, after death, the properties they possessed during life. The properties of the vital solids disappear directly death occurs. Hence the simple solids have fewer diseases, and their maladies admit of easy classification. The real difficulty lies in the vital solids. Cullen made the nervous system the basis of his pathology; and assigned the chief place to an occult principle, which he termed the animal power, or energy, of the brain. This principle acted on the vital solids. When it worked well, the body was healthy; when it worked ill, the body was unhealthy. The influences acting on this energy were either physical or mental. The physical were heat, cold, and effluvia; the mental were the will, the emotions, the appetites, the propensities, and habit and imitation.

This one-sided solid philosophy corrected the error of the pathologists, from Galen downward, who laid too much emphasis on the liquids. The old pathology was pernicious, because its chief remedy was bleeding, which weakened those it was unable to slay. Solid pathology was the first effective barrier against this. Cullen's doctrine of fever will illustrate his application of the method. The cause of fever, he says, is diminished energy of the brain, produced by sedatives like effluvia, marsh or human, intemperance, fear, and cold. The disease passes rapidly through the nervous system; appearing first in a chill, or cold fit, accompanied by a spasm at the extremities of the arteries where they touch the surface of the body. This irritates heart and arteries, till the spasm is relaxed. Increased heart action restores the brain energy; the system rallies; the extreme vessels are relieved; sweat is excreted, and the fever abates. Shutting out all consideration of bodily fluids, the successive stages of fever, languor, cold fit, and hot fit, might be generalized by reasoning exclusively from the solids. A similar process of thought gave birth to his *Nosology*, or general classification of diseases, which is, however, now falling into disrepute.

John Hunter's only fault was an occasional obscurity, not merely of language, but also of thought. His understanding at times seems troubled by the grandeur of its own conceptions, and doubts what path it ought to take. He hesitated; the utterance of his intellect became indistinct. Yet among the great masters of organic science he belongs to the same rank as Aristotle, Harvey, and Bichat, and is superior to Haller or Cuvier.

Hunter remained in Scotland till the age of twenty, when he settled in London. His early associations were deductive; the later environment was inductive. His work represents both methods. Among his most impressive discoveries, based upon his indefatigable collection of facts, are, the true nature of the circulation of crustacea and insects; the organ of hearing in cephalopods; the mollusks' power of absorbing their shells; the fact that bees secrete wax, and do not collect it; the semicircular canals of the cetacea; the lymphatics of birds; and the air-cells in the bones of birds. He anticipated the recent discoveries in the embryo of the kangaroo, and he proved the muscularity of the arteries, of the iris, and the digestion of the stomach after death by its own juice. He followed the blood in the embryo, and established that red corpuscles are formed later than the other components. He inferred from this that the purpose of the red corpuscles was to minister to the strength of the system, rather than to its repair—a principle now universally admitted.

Hunter now turned to the vegetable world, to see if he could not detect some law, common to animal and vegetable, which should unite both. He pointed out that the capacity of action is of three kinds, the first being the action of the individual upon the materials it already possesses. This gives rise to growth, secretion, and other functions, in which the juice of the plant is equivalent to the blood of the animal. The second kind of action had for its object to increase these materials: it was always excited by want, and its result was to nourish and preserve the individual. The third kind was due to external causes, including the whole material world, all the phenomena of which were stimuli to some kind of action. Though animals could do many things which plants could not, the immediate cause of action in both is the same. In animals there is more variety of motion; in plants, more real power. A horse is stronger than a man; yet a small vine can not only support, but can raise a column of fluid five times higher than a horse can.

Hunter was led to consider how motion is produced by various forces, such as magnetism, electricity, gravitation, and chemical attraction. This carried him into inorganic science, where he saw that the foundations of organic science must be laid. He aimed to unite all the branches of physical science. His study of crystals, regular and irregular as well, pointed out to him that nature, even in the midst of her deviations, still retains her regularity. Or, as he elsewhere puts it, deviation is, under certain circumstances, part of the law of nature. To generalize these irregularities, or, in other words, to show that they were not irregularities at all, was the main object of Hunter's life. He studied the aberrations of structure and function, in the vegetable as well as the animal world. Aberrations of form he carried down into the mineral kingdom. His work places him at the head of all pathologists, ancient or modern. For, with him, the science of pathology did not mean the laws of disease in man alone, or among animals alone, or even in the whole kingdom of life; it covered the whole material world, lifeless as well as living. His object was to raise a science of the abnormal.

His love of deduction at times showed itself, as in the ultimate principle he propounded, that diseases move more rapidly toward the skin than toward internal parts, by virtue of some hidden force, which also obliges vegetables to approach the surface of the earth. Another principle was, that in no substance, be it what it may, can two processes go on in the same part at the same time. We know that this is erroneous. It is well to remember that Plato failed in induction, and Bacon in deduction. Only Aristotle and Newton combined both with equal ability. In Hunter, the understanding was troubled by the conflict between the two. Yet to him may be traced all the surgical improvements introduced during the forty years after his death.

He was in the midst of a people who had no sympathy with deduction. His English contemporaries, prudent, sagacious, but short-sighted, were unable to appreciate his comprehensive speculations. They regarded him as little more than an innovator and enthusiast. The great Scotchman, thrown among a nation whose habit of mind differed from his own, stood in a position of solitary and comfortless superiority.

This concludes the investigation of the Scotch intellect as it unfolded in the seventeenth and eighteenth centuries. The monkish literature of the seventeenth century differed much from the scientific and philosophic literature of the eighteenth: yet they had this in common, that both were deductive. Both reasoned from assumed general principles down to facts, instead of reasoning inductively from facts upward to theories. The inductive reasoner starts with facts the mass of people are familiar with, so that they can follow his upward steps. The deductive thinker begins with vast theoretical generalizations which cannot interest the people, so that he loses their interest from the start. An inductive philosophy is more likely to be widely diffused than a deductive one. For one person who can think, there are a hundred who can observe. The deductive method, hidden from the public gaze, can never command the public sympathy.

The only exception to this is theology, the theory of religion. Science is the result of inquiry; theology, the result of faith. The spirit of doubt rules the one; the spirit of belief, the other. In science originality is the parent of discovery; in theology it is the parent of heresy, and a fault, rather than a merit. The brilliant deductive thinking of the Scotchmen of the eighteenth century produced little or no effect on the nation at large. In France and England, the prevailing philosophy was inductive, and affected not only the intellectual classes, but the popular mind.

Except for the *Wealth of Nations,* none of the products considered perceptibly influenced public opinion. This exception was because Adam Smith's work restricted the power of rulers so fully, and gave such wide powers to the people. As a democratic book, it found favor in Scotland. Barring this, the rest of the literature did not affect the people, and did nothing to decrease their load of superstitions. In Scotland to-day the man of unorthodox opinions is worse off than anywhere except in Spain. Thus in 1853 the cholera ravaged Scotland. The remedy was to feed the poor, to cleanse the cesspools, to ventilate the houses. The misguided clergy instead ordered a national fast, which would have brought the disease to thousands of already enfeebled persons. This was to be accompanied by a public humiliation, and a thunder of religious denunciations of the sins of the land. The Scotch clergy called on England to help in this superstitious act. Lord Palmerston, to whom this call was addressed, wrote back, reminding the Scotch that the affairs of this world are regulated by natural laws. One of these laws of the spread of disease refers to the exhalations of bodies, which spreads contagion by crowding. He advised the Presbytery that it was better to cleanse than to fast. If they did not cleanse themselves now, the pestilence would revisit them, "in spite of all the prayers and fastings of a united but in-active nation."

This correspondence illustrates the terrible struggle between theology and science, which began with the persecution of science by the church, and to-day is evidenced by the destruction of theological beliefs by science. It is time that superstitious notions should come to an end. Men will cease to be terrified by phantoms which their own ignorance has reared. This age may not witness the emancipation; but it will come, and perhaps sooner than is expected. The ancient empire must crumble; the dominion of superstition, already decaying, will crumble into dust. It will be clearly seen that from the beginning there has been no discrepancy, no disorder, no interference; but that all the events which surround us, even to the furthest limits of the material creation, are but different parts of a single scheme, which is filled with one glorious principle of universal and undeviating regularity.

dilletantism — T+B